Chinese Cuisine

2 Books In 1: 125 Recipes Cookbook
For Dim Sum Bao Dumplings And
Delicious Dishes From China

Maki Blanc

CHINESE

COOKBOOK

Authentic Dishes from China in 60 Recipes.

Maki Blanc

CONTENTS

Introduction

"The best place to live would definitely be America but the best place to eat will always be China".

The expression is a demonstration of the fame of Chinese food all over the planet. Food is a significant part of culture for Chinese individuals. Chinese appreciate eating as well as believe that eating great food can bring happiness and satisfaction to the family and connections.

Chinese food varies from one area to another according to the environment and individuals that are native to those districts. The sodden, sticky environment of the west brings about zesty hot food from Sichuan, where Sichuan chilies and peppercorns are added to recipes in huge amounts. Individuals in the waterfront districts of Guangzhou and Fujian are honored with copious produce from the ocean, and the environment favors rice cultivation, so lighter rice and fish dishes are transcendently from these areas. The north of China is cold and dry and hardier plants, for example, cabbage and wheat mostly develop there; subsequently, dumplings, and noodle dishes come from there.

Chinese individuals overall are not as worried about nourishment as individuals do in Western culture. They are more worried about the food's color, flavor, and fragrance. These are the essential focuses for great Chinese cooking. Chinese suppers comprise of four nutrition types: grains, fruits, vegetables, and meat. On account of lactose intolerance, Chinese do not consume a lot of dairy items.

Chinese individuals will change their menus with the switch of each season, from the unrefined components to the cooking techniques; each season utilizes various flavors that go with the dishes. Winter has a thicker and rich flavor, while summer highlights in light and cool flavors. Cooking styles in winter are generally braised or stewed, while in summer, they are for the most part filled in as cold and dressed with sauce.

All things considered, Chinese substitute dairy and its products with soymilk and tofu, which likewise contain a lot of protein and calcium. Western treats like treats, cakes, pies, and frozen yogurt are eaten uniquely on extraordinary events like birthday celebrations and weddings. After supper, families generally eat occasional natural product as pastry. Chinese pastries, for example, red bean soup, seed soup, or papaya soup are served sometimes as a unique treat on a warm summer's evening.

This book contains 60 flavorful recipes belonging to dessert, stinky tofu, stir-fry, bao buns, dumplings, noodle soups, spring rolls, dry noodles and many other categories. You should be all ready to cook authentic Chinese food with this cookbook by your side. So, keep reading!

The 60 Chinese Recipes You Need To Know

Chinese dishes are very yummy, full of nutrition and do not take much time to cook. You should definitely try these recipes. You will not be disappointed!

ALMOND COOKIES

INGREDIENTS

- Two whole eggs
- One and a half cup of almond flour
- A pinch of kosher salt
- One cup of unsalted butter
- One cup of sugar
- Two tablespoons of all-purpose flour
- Half teaspoon of baking soda
- One teaspoon of almond extract
- Thinly sliced almonds for garnishing

COOK TIME: 15 mins
SERVING: 60

INSTRUCTIONS

1. Preheat the oven to 220 degrees.
2. Take a bowl.
3. Add the eggs and almond extract into the bowl.
4. Mix the ingredients well until the mixture turns fluffy.
5. Add the butter, baking soda, sugar, almond flour, salt and all-purpose flour into the bowl.
6. Mix the ingredients well.
7. Knead the dough and roll it out into a semi thick sheet.
8. Cut round cookies out of the dough using a cutter and sprinkle the almonds on top.
9. Take a baking tray.
10. Grease the tray well and add the cookies on the baking tray.
11. Make sure you flat the cookie batter and then place it in the oven.
12. Bake the cookies for fifteen minutes or until light golden brown in color.
13. Dish out when done.
14. Your dish is ready to be served.

ASIAN CHOPPED SALAD

INGREDIENTS

- One cup of finely chopped scallions
- One cup of chopped snap peas
- One cup of chopped purple cabbage
- One cup of bean sprouts
- One cup of red bell pepper
- Half teaspoon of salt
- One teaspoon of grated ginger
- Two cups of cucumber
- A quarter cup of rice vinegar
- One teaspoon of minced garlic
- One tablespoon of soy sauce
- Two tablespoons of maple syrup
- One teaspoon of red chili paste
- Two tbsp. of sesame seeds
- Two tablespoons of toasted sesame oil
- Chopped almonds for garnishing

INSTRUCTIONS

1. Take a large bowl.
2. Add the red chili paste, soy sauce, red vinegar, ginger, garlic and maple syrup into the bowl.
3. Mix the ingredients well.
4. Add the bean sprouts, cucumber, scallions, snap peas, cabbage and red bell pepper into the bowl.
5. Divide the chopped salad into four serving bowls.
6. Add the soy sauce mixture on top of the chopped salad.
7. Mix well.
8. Add the sesame seeds, almonds and sesame oil on top.
9. Serve.

Tip: You can toast the almonds. It will add crunchiness to the salad.

COOK TIME: *5 mins*
SERVING: *4*

BANG BANG CHICKEN

INGREDIENTS

- One cup of buttermilk
- Half cup of cornstarch
- Vegetable oil for frying
- One tablespoon of hot sauce
- One cup of all-purpose flour
- Salt to taste
- Black pepper to taste
- One egg
- One cup of panko
- One pound of boneless chicken pieces
- **For sauce:**
- One tablespoon of sweet chili sauce
- A quarter cup of mayonnaise
- One tablespoon of hot sauce
- One tablespoon of honey

INSTRUCTIONS

1. Take a mixing bowl.
2. Add the buttermilk, egg, salt, black pepper, hot sauce and cornstarch into the bowl.
3. Add the chicken pieces in the bowl and mix well.
4. Take a frying pan.
5. Add the oil into the pan and heat it well.
6. Cover the chicken pieces in the panko crumbs and add them into the oil.
7. Cook the chicken pieces well and dish them out when they turn golden brown in color.
8. Take a bowl.
9. Add the honey, mayonnaise, sweet chili sauce and hot sauce into the bowl.
10. Mix the ingredients well and drizzle the sauce over the chicken pieces.
11. Your dish is ready to be served.

Tip: You can use any bread crumbs if panko is unavailable

COOK TIME: 20 mins
SERVING: 4

BEEF AND GREEN ONION DUMPLING

INGREDIENTS

- One cup of all-purpose flour
- Half cup of water
- Two cups of minced beef
- Two cups of chopped green onions
- Two teaspoons of shaoxing wine
- Half cup of stock
- One teaspoon of Sichuan peppercorns
- One teaspoon of garlic powder
- One teaspoon of ginger powder
- One tablespoon of oyster sauce
- One teaspoon of sesame oil
- One tablespoon of soy sauce
- Salt to taste
- Black pepper to taste
- Garlic dipping sauce for serving

COOK TIME: 20 mins
SERVING: 4

INSTRUCTIONS

1. Take a large bowl.
2. Add the flour, salt and water in a bowl.
3. Mix the dough and knead the ingredients well.
4. Keep aside.
5. Take a pan.
6. Add the oil, beef mince, green onions, soy sauce, oyster sauce, stock, shaoxing wine, Sichuan peppercorns, ginger powder, garlic powder, black pepper, and salt into the pan.
7. Cook the mixture well until the ingredients are done.
8. Roll out the dough into a thin sheet.
9. Cut small round circles in the dough.
10. Add the cooked filling in the circle and shape it out in the form of a dumpling.
11. Take a large steamer.
12. Add the dumplings into the pan.
13. Steam them well until the dumplings are done.
14. Your dish is ready to be served with garlic dipping sauce.

BOILED PORK DUMPLINGS

INGREDIENTS

- Dumpling wrapper as required
- A quarter cup of chopped scallions
- Two cups of minced pork
- One cup of cabbage
- Two teaspoons of shaoxing wine
- Half cup of stock
- One teaspoon of garlic powder
- One teaspoon of ginger powder
- One teaspoon of sesame oil
- Salt to taste
- Black pepper to taste
- Spicy sauce for serving

INSTRUCTIONS

1. Take a pan.
2. Add the oil, scallions, pork mince, cabbage, stock, shaoxing wine, ginger powder, garlic powder, black pepper, and salt into the pan.
3. Cook the mixture well until the ingredients are done.
4. Add the pork filling in the wrappers and shape each of them in the form of a dumpling.
5. Take a large sauce pan.
6. Add water into the pan and close the lid.
7. Let it boil.
8. Add the dumplings into the pan and boil for five to ten minutes.
9. Dish out when the dumplings are done.
10. Your dish is ready to be served with spicy sauce.

COOK TIME: 20 mins
SERVING: 4

BEEF AND BLACK BEANS BAO BUNS

INGREDIENTS

- Half cup of water
- One teaspoon of dry yeast
- A quarter cup of milk
- One tablespoon of cane sugar
- A quarter cup of butter
- Three cups of all-purpose flour
- **For filling:**
- One pound of beef mince
- One teaspoon of garlic powder
- One teaspoon of ginger powder
- One tablespoon of dark soy sauce
- One teaspoon of oyster sauce
- Two tablespoons of rice vinegar
- One cup of black bean sauce
- Salt to taste
- Black pepper to taste
- One tablespoon of cooking oil

COOK TIME: *30 mins*
SERVING: *4*

INSTRUCTIONS

1. Take a mixing bowl.
2. Add the water in the pan and bring it to boil.
3. Remove it from heat.
4. Add the sugar and yeast into the water and dissolve it.
5. Add the milk, all-purpose flour, and butter into the bowl.
6. Mix well and knead it properly for ten minutes.
7. Put aside.
8. Take a pan.
9. Add the oil in it and heat well.
10. Add the beef mince, ginger powder, salt, black pepper, and garlic powder in it.
11. Mix well and add the rice vinegar, dark soy sauce and oyster sauce into the mixture.
12. Make oval bao buns from the dough.
13. Place the buns in a steamer to get steamed.
14. Dish out the bao buns after thirty minutes.
15. Cut the bao buns in between and add the cooked mixture in it.
16. Drizzle the black bean sauce on top of the mixture.
17. Your dish is ready to be served.

BEEF AND ONION STIR FRY

INGREDIENTS

- A quarter cup of oyster sauce
- A pound of beef strips
- Two teaspoons of grated garlic
- Two teaspoons of grated ginger
- Two teaspoons of soy sauce
- One teaspoon of sugar
- Half pound of sliced onions
- Two tablespoons of cornstarch
- Two tablespoons of toasted sesame oil
- Black pepper to taste
- Salt to taste
- Cooked rice for serving

COOK TIME: 30 mins
SERVING: 4

INSTRUCTIONS

1. Take a mixing bowl.
2. Add the soy sauce, oyster sauce, sugar and cornstarch into the bowl.
3. Mix well and place it aside.
4. Take a large pan.
5. Add the oil into the pan and heat it well.
6. Add the onions into the pan.
7. Cook well and then add the ginger and garlic paste.
8. Add the beef strips into the pan.
9. Season the strips with salt and black pepper.
10. Cook the beef until it begins to turn white.
11. Add the cornstarch mixture into the pan.
12. Mix well and cook for five minutes.
13. Dish out the stir-fry and serve with cooked rice.

CHINESE LAMB MEATBALLS HOYPOT

INGREDIENTS

- One tablespoon of brown sugar
- Two tablespoons of vegetable oil
- Two tablespoons of soy sauce
- Half pound of frozen lamb meatballs
- Half cup of chopped onions
- Two tablespoons of lime juice
- A quarter cup of chili sauce
- One cup of diced tofu
- One cup of Napa cabbage
- Black pepper to taste
- Half cup of red bell pepper
- One cup of button mushrooms
- Half teaspoon of grated ginger
- Half teaspoon of grated garlic

INSTRUCTIONS

1. Heat the oil in a stockpot.
2. Add the onion into the pot.
3. Cook and stir for three minutes.
4. Add the meatballs, tofu and vegetables into the pot.
5. Add the stock, curry paste, soy sauce, brown sugar, garlic, and ginger into the pot.
6. Reduce the heat to low, cover, and leave to simmer for twenty minutes.
7. Dish out the hotpot and add the lime juice on top.
8. Your dish is ready to be served.

COOK TIME: 15 mins
SERVING: 2

CHICKEN CHOP SUOY

INGREDIENTS

- Two tablespoons of Sichuan pepper
- A quarter cup of chopped scallions
- Two cups of chicken strips
- Two teaspoons of shaoxing wine
- Half cup of stock
- One teaspoon of garlic powder
- One teaspoon of ginger powder
- One teaspoon of sesame oil
- Salt to taste
- Black pepper to taste
- **For Suoy:**
- Two cups of mixed vegetables
- Half teaspoon of sesame oil
- One teaspoon of soy sauce
- Two cups of chicken stock
- Black pepper to taste
- Salt to taste
- Two tablespoons of Chinese cinnamon
- Spring onion for serving
- Toasted sesame seeds for serving

COOK TIME: 20 mins
SERVING: 4

INSTRUCTIONS

1. Take a pan.
2. Add the oil, scallions, chicken strips, Sichuan peppers, stock, shaoxing wine, ginger powder, garlic powder, black pepper, and salt into the pan.
3. Cook the mixture well until the ingredients are done.
4. Dish out the chicken mixture.
5. Add the vegetables and rest of the ingredients of the suoy in the pan.
6. Cook the ingredients well.
7. Add the chicken strips into the pan.
8. Cook them well until the liquid is reduced.
9. Garnish the chop suoy with spring onion and sesame seeds.
10. Your dish is ready to be served.

CHINESE MAYONNAISE AND SHRIMP DUMPLINGS

INGREDIENTS

- Dumpling wrappers as required
- A quarter cup of chopped scallions
- Two cups of minced shrimp
- One cup of mayonnaise
- Two teaspoons of shaoxing wine
- Half cup of stock
- One teaspoon of dried shrimp
- One teaspoon of garlic powder
- One teaspoon of ginger powder
- Oil for frying
- Salt to taste
- Black pepper to taste

COOK TIME: 20 mins
SERVING: 4

INSTRUCTIONS

1. Take a pan.
2. Add the oil, scallions, shrimp mince, mayonnaise, stock, shaoxing wine, dried shrimp, ginger powder, garlic powder, black pepper, and salt into the pan.
3. Cook the mixture well until the ingredients are done.
4. Add the shrimp filling in each of the wrappers and shape them out in the form of dumplings.
5. Take a large frying pan.
6. Add the oil into the pan and heat it well.
7. Add the dumplings into the pan and deep fry them.
8. Cook them well until they turn golden brown.
9. Your dish is ready to be served.

CHICKEN DUMPLINGS WITH SHIITAKE MUSHROOMS

INGREDIENTS

- Dumpling wrappers as required
- A quarter cup of chopped scallions
- Two cups of ground chicken
- One cup of chopped shiitake mushrooms
- Two teaspoons of shaoxing wine
- One teaspoon of garlic powder
- One teaspoon of ginger powder
- One tablespoon of sugar
- One teaspoon of sesame oil
- Salt to taste
- Black pepper to taste
- Dipping sauce for serving

INSTRUCTIONS

1. Take a pan.
2. Add the oil, scallions, chicken, mushrooms, sugar, shaoxing wine, ginger powder, garlic powder, black pepper, and salt into the pan.
3. Cook the mixture well until the ingredients are done.
4. Add the cooked filling in the wrappers and shape them out in the form of dumplings.
5. Take a large frying pan.
6. Add the sesame oil and dumplings into the pan.
7. Add a quarter cup of water into the pan and close the lid.
8. Cook well until the dumplings are done.
9. Your dish is ready to be served with dipping sauce.

COOK TIME: 20 mins
SERVING: 4

CHINESE BEEF AND BROCCOLI SOUP

INGREDIENTS

- Two cups of broccoli florets
- Six cups of beef broth
- Half cup of beef mince
- One cup of chopped onions
- Two teaspoons of minced garlic
- Two teaspoons of minced ginger
- Two tablespoons of corn starch
- A quarter cup of soy sauce
- A quarter cup of oyster sauce
- Half cup of chopped green onions
- Two teaspoons of black pepper
- Two and a half tablespoon of coconut oil
- Salt to taste
- Chopped green onions for serving

COOK TIME: *30 mins*
SERVING: *2*

INSTRUCTIONS

1. Take a sauce pan.
2. Add the coconut oil, and beef mince into the pan.
3. Cook well for five to ten minutes.
4. Add the onions, garlic and ginger into the pan.
5. Cook until they are golden brown, then add stock when they turn golden brown.
6. Add the broccoli, soy sauce, and oyster sauce into the pan.
7. Boil the mixture well.
8. Add the corn starch, salt and black pepper into the mixture.
9. Cook the ingredients until done and dish out into two bowls.
10. Add the spring onions on top.
11. Your dish is ready to be served.

Tip: You can substitute ground beef with shredded beef strips.

CORIANDER AND SHRIMP BAO BUNS

INGREDIENTS

- Half cup of water
- One teaspoon of dry yeast
- A quarter cup of milk
- One tablespoon of cane sugar
- A quarter cup of butter
- Three cups of all-purpose flour
- **For filling:**
- One pound of shrimp mince
- One teaspoon of garlic powder
- One teaspoon of ginger powder
- A quarter cup of chopped coriander
- One tablespoon of sugar
- One tablespoon of dark soy sauce
- One teaspoon of oyster sauce
- Salt to taste
- Black pepper to taste
- One tablespoon of cooking oil

COOK TIME: 30 mins
SERVING: 4

INSTRUCTIONS

1. Take a mixing bowl.
2. Add the water in the pan and bring it to boil.
3. Remove it from heat.
4. Add the sugar and yeast into the water and dissolve it.
5. Add the milk, all-purpose flour, and butter into the bowl.
6. Mix well and knead it properly for ten minutes.
7. Take a pan.
8. Add the oil in it and heat well.
9. Add the shrimp mince, ginger powder, sugar, coriander, salt, black pepper, and garlic powder in it.
10. Mix well and add the dark soy sauce and oyster sauce into the mixture.
11. Make oval bao buns from the dough and add the shrimp mince in the middle of the buns.
12. Place the buns in a steamer to get steamed.
13. Dish out the bao buns after thirty minutes.
14. Your dish is ready to be served.

CLASSIC SPRING ONION, RADISH AND LOTUS STEM CHINESE SALAD

INGREDIENTS

- One cup of finely chopped lotus root stem
- One cup of cooked pork loins
- One cup of chopped pickled radish
- One cup of cooked shrimp
- One cup of chopped spring onion
- Half teaspoon of salt
- One teaspoon of grated ginger
- A quarter cup of rice vinegar
- One teaspoon of minced garlic
- One tablespoon of soy sauce
- Two tablespoons of lime juice
- Two tablespoons of sesame seeds
- Two tablespoons of toasted sesame oil

INSTRUCTIONS

1. Take a large bowl.
2. Add the sesame oil, salt, soy sauce, rice vinegar, ginger, garlic and lime juice into the bowl.
3. Mix the ingredients well.
4. Add the lotus root stem, pickled radish, cooked shrimp, pork loins and chopped spring onion into the bowl.
5. Divide the salad into four serving bowls.
6. Add the sesame sauce mixture on top of the chopped salad.
7. Mix well.
8. Add the sesame seeds on top.
9. Serve.

COOK TIME: *5 mins*
SERVING: *4*

CRISPY TOFU NOODLE SALAD

INGREDIENTS

- Two cups of tofu pieces
- A quarter cup of corn starch
- Salt to taste
- Two tablespoons of sesame oil
- **For dressing:**
- Two tablespoons of sliced red pepper
- Two tablespoons of crushed garlic
- A quarter cup of chopped spring onion
- One tablespoon of light soy sauce
- Two tablespoons of black vinegar
- One tablespoon of sugar
- Salt to taste
- Black pepper to taste
- Two tablespoons of sesame oil
- Two cups of boiled noodles

COOK TIME: 5 mins
SERVING: 4

INSTRUCTIONS

1. Mix the tofu and Take a pan.
2. Add the sesame oil into the pan.
3. Add the tofu pieces, corn starch and cook them for five minutes.
4. Season them with salt and dish out.
5. Take a bowl.
6. Add the sesame oil, crushed garlic, sliced red chili, black vinegar, spring onion, soy sauce, black pepper, and sugar into the bowl.
7. Mix the ingredients well.
8. Dish out the tofu pieces when they are almost done.
9. Drizzle the prepared dressing on top of the okra pieces.
10. Toss the noodles into the mixture and add into a serving dish.
11. Your dish is ready to be served.

CHINESE FRESH TOMATOES AND SPINACH SALAD

INGREDIENTS

- Two cups of diced tomatoes
- Two cups of chopped spinach
- Half cup of roasted peanuts
- Half cup of dried shrimps
- **For dressing:**
- Two tablespoons of shallot crisps
- A quarter cup of chopped spring onion
- One tablespoon of cayenne pepper powder
- Two tablespoons of black vinegar
- One tablespoon of sugar
- Salt to taste
- Black pepper to taste
- Two tablespoons of sesame oil

COOK TIME: 20 mins
SERVING: 2

INSTRUCTIONS

1. Add the tomatoes, spinach, dried shrimps and roasted peanuts into the large bowl.
2. Take a bowl.
3. Add the shallot crisps, cayenne pepper powder, black vinegar, spring onion, soy sauce, black pepper, and sugar into the bowl.
4. Mix the ingredients well.
5. Drizzle the prepared dressing on top of the tomato mixture.
6. Toss the mixture and add into a serving dish.
7. Your dish is ready to be served.

CHINESE COLD SESAME NOODLES

INGREDIENTS

- One cup of finely chopped scallions
- One cup of chopped carrots
- One cup of grated cucumber
- One cup of chopped purple cabbage
- One cup of bean sprouts
- One cup of crushed peanuts
- Half teaspoon of salt
- One teaspoon of grated ginger
- Two cups of boiled noodles
- A quarter cup of peanut butter
- One teaspoon of minced garlic
- One tablespoon of soy sauce
- Two tablespoons of Chinese sesame paste
- One teaspoon of orange juice
- Two tablespoons of toasted sesame seeds

COOK TIME: 5 mins
SERVING: 4

INSTRUCTIONS

1. Take a large bowl.
2. Add the peanut butter, soy sauce, sesame paste, ginger, garlic and orange juice into the bowl.
3. Mix the ingredients well.
4. Add the bean sprouts, noodles, scallions, peanuts, cabbage and cucumber in another bowl.
5. Divide the chopped salad into four serving bowls.
6. Add the peanut butter mixture on top of the chopped salad.
7. Mix well.
8. Add the sesame seeds on top.
9. Serve.

CHICKEN SHANGHAI NOODLES

INGREDIENTS

- Three packs of boiled shanghai style noodles
- One pound of chicken strips
- Two cups of cabbage
- One teaspoon of minced garlic
- One cup of grated carrots
- Half cup of green onions
- Two tablespoons of vegetable oil
- **For sauce:**
- A quarter cup of chicken broth
- One tablespoon of cornstarch
- Two teaspoons of Chinese dry sherry
- Half cup of soy sauce
- One tablespoon of hoisin sauce
- Half teaspoon of granulated sugar

COOK TIME: 20 mins
SERVING: 8

INSTRUCTIONS

1. Take a bowl.
2. Mix the hoisin sauce, chicken broth, Chinese dry sherry, cornstarch, soy sauce and sugar to make sauce.
3. Keep aside.
4. Take a pan and add the oil into the pan.
5. Add the garlic, chicken pieces, carrot, and cabbage into the pan.
6. Cook the ingredients well for fifteen minutes and add the sauce into the mixture.
7. Mix the ingredients well.
8. Add the noodles, and green onions into the mixture.
9. Stir fry and dish out.
10. Serve hot.

CHINESE PEKING DUCK WITH SIRARCHA SAUCE

INGREDIENTS

- A quarter cup of plum sirarcha sauce
- One teaspoon of garlic powder
- Two teaspoons of paprika
- Two teaspoons of salt
- One teaspoon of black pepper
- Two pounds of whole duck
- Half cup of garlic cloves
- Fresh herbs
- Half cup of diced onions

COOK TIME: 2 hours
SERVING: 4

INSTRUCTIONS

1. Take a bowl.
2. Add the plum sirarcha sauce, garlic powder, salt, black pepper, and paprika into the bowl.
3. Mix well.
4. Take a baking tray.
5. Make sure you grease the tray properly.
6. Place the duck on the tray.
7. Add the garlic cloves, herb and diced onions into the cavity of the duck.
8. Cover the duck with the prepared sauce.
9. Preheat the oven at 150 degrees.
10. Place the duck into the oven for two hours.
11. Dish out when the duck is done.
12. Your dish is ready to be served.

CRISPY CHICKEN BAO BUNS WITH SLAW

INGREDIENTS

- Half cup of water
- One teaspoon of dry yeast
- A quarter cup of milk
- One tablespoon of cane sugar
- A quarter cup of butter
- Three cups of all-purpose flour
- **For filling:**
- One pound of crispy chicken pieces
- Two cups of coleslaw

COOK TIME: 20 mins
SERVING: 4

INSTRUCTIONS

1. Take a pan.
2. Add the water in the pan and bring it to boil.
3. Remove it from heat.
4. Add the sugar and yeast into the water and dissolve it.
5. Add the milk, all-purpose flour, and butter into the bowl.
6. Mix well and knead it properly for ten minutes.
7. Make oval bao buns from the dough and place them in a steamer to get steamed.
8. Dish out the bao buns after thirty minutes.
9. Cut in the middle and add the crispy chicken and coleslaw in it.
10. Your dish is ready to be served.

DIM SUM SPRING ROLLS

INGREDIENTS

- One teaspoon of sesame oil
- One cup of chopped onions
- One cup of grated carrots
- One cup of sliced red cabbage
- One cup of bamboo shoots
- Salt to taste
- Half teaspoon of corn starch
- Two tablespoons of rice vinegar
- Three tablespoons of soy sauce
- Eight spring roll wrappers
- Cooking oil for frying

COOK TIME: 5 mins
SERVING: 4

INSTRUCTIONS

1. Take a bowl.
2. Add the corn starch, bamboo shoots, red cabbage, carrots, salt, rice vinegar and soy sauce into a bowl.
3. Mix well.
4. Add the formed mixture into the roll wrappers.
5. Fold the wrappers into a roll.
6. Take a pan.
7. Add the oil and heat it well.
8. Add the rolls into the oil and fry until they turn golden brown on all sides.
9. Dish out.
10. Serve the spring rolls with any sauce of your choice.

FIVE SPICE CAKE

INGREDIENTS

- Dumpling wrappers as required
- A quarter cup of chopped scallions
- Two cups of mixed vegetables
- Two teaspoons of shaoxing wine
- Half cup of stock
- One tablespoon of sugar
- A quarter cup of soy sauce
- One teaspoon of garlic powder
- One teaspoon of ginger powder
- Oil for frying
- Salt to taste
- White pepper to taste

INSTRUCTIONS

1. Take a pan.
2. Add the oil, scallions, soy sauce, mixed vegetables, stock, shaoxing wine, ginger powder, garlic powder, sugar, white pepper, and salt into the pan.
3. Cook the mixture well until the ingredients are done.
4. Add the cooked filling in the wrappers and shape them out in the form of a dumpling.
5. Take a large frying pan.
6. Add the oil into the pan and heat it well.
7. Add the dumplings into the pan and deep fry them.
8. Cook them well until they turn golden brown.
9. Your dish is ready to be served.

COOK TIME: 20 mins
SERVING: 4

FRIED VEGETABLE DUMPLINGS

INGREDIENTS

- Dumpling wrappers as required
- A quarter cup of chopped scallions
- Two cups of mixed vegetables
- Two teaspoons of shaoxing wine
- Half cup of stock
- One tablespoon of sugar
- A quarter cup of soy sauce
- One teaspoon of garlic powder
- One teaspoon of ginger powder
- Oil for frying
- Salt to taste
- White pepper to taste

COOK TIME: 20 mins
SERVING: 4

INSTRUCTIONS

1. Take a pan.
2. Add the oil, scallions, soy sauce, mixed vegetables, stock, shaoxing wine, ginger powder, garlic powder, sugar, white pepper, and salt into the pan.
3. Cook the mixture well until the ingredients are done.
4. Add the cooked filling in the wrappers and shape them out in the form of a dumpling.
5. Take a large frying pan.
6. Add the oil into the pan and heat it well.
7. Add the dumplings into the pan and deep fry them.
8. Cook them well until they turn golden brown.
9. Your dish is ready to be served.

FRIED BANANAS

INGREDIENTS

- Half teaspoon of cinnamon powder
- One pound of banana slices
- One tablespoon of coconut oil

COOK TIME: 20 mins
SERVING: 8

INSTRUCTIONS

1. Take a bowl.
2. Mix the cinnamon powder and banana slices into the bowl.
3. Mix well and keep aside.
4. Take a pan and add the coconut oil into the pan.
5. Add the banana slices in the pan.
6. Cook the banana slices well for fifteen minutes on both sides.
7. Dish out when done.
8. Serve hot.

Tip: Do not make this recipe using over ripe banana slices

GRILLED LAMB MEATBALLS

INGREDIENTS

- Half cup of chopped onions
- Salt to taste
- Black pepper to taste
- One pound of lamb mince
- One teaspoon of chopped parsley
- One tablespoon of ground cumin
- A quarter teaspoon of ground garlic
- One teaspoon of chopped cilantro
- A quarter teaspoon of ground paprika
- One egg
- Two tablespoons of sesame oil
- Cooked rice for serving

INSTRUCTIONS

1. Take a grill pan.
2. Heat it.
3. Take a mixing bowl.
4. Add the lamb mince, onions, salt, garlic, black pepper, parsley eggs, paprika, cumin, sesame oil and cilantro in the bowl.
5. Mix well.
6. Make small bite sized meatballs from the mixture.
7. Place the meatballs on the grill pan and grill them.
8. Dish out when they turn golden brown in color.
9. Your dish is ready to be served with cooked rice.

.

COOK TIME: *20 mins*
SERVING: *4*

GENERAL TSO'S CHICKEN

INGREDIENTS

- Two tablespoons of cornstarch
- One pound of chicken cubes
- One teaspoon of baking soda
- Two teaspoons of soy sauce
- One teaspoon of Shaoxing wine
- Two tablespoons of vegetable oil
- Green onions for serving
- **For sauce:**
- A quarter cup of water
- Half cup of oyster sauce
- Half cup of soy sauce
- One teaspoon of grated ginger
- One teaspoon of grated garlic
- A quarter teaspoon of rice vinegar

COOK TIME: 20 mins
SERVING: 4

INSTRUCTIONS

1. Take a bowl.
2. Mix the water, grated ginger, red pepper flakes, oyster sauce, grated garlic, and soy sauce to make sauce.
3. Keep aside.
4. Take a bowl.
5. Add the cornstarch, chicken pieces, baking soda, soy sauce and Shaoxing wine into the bowl.
6. Mix well.
7. Take a pan and add the vegetable oil into the pan.
8. Add the chicken cubes and stir fry the chicken in the oil until they turn crispy.
9. Dish out the chicken when done.
10. Add the sauce and chicken into the mixture.
11. Mix the ingredients well.
12. Add the green onions into the mixture.
13. Stir fry for five minutes and dish out.
14. Serve hot.

GRILLED CHICKEN MEATBALLS

INGREDIENTS

- One pound of chicken mince
- Half cup of chopped onions
- Salt to taste
- Black pepper to taste
- One teaspoon of chopped parsley
- A quarter teaspoon of ground garlic
- One teaspoon of chopped cilantro
- A quarter cup of panko
- One egg
- Two tablespoons of sesame oil
- BBQ sauce for serving

COOK TIME: 20 mins
SERVING: 4

INSTRUCTIONS

1. Take a grill pan.
2. Heat it.
3. Take a mixing bowl.
4. Add the chicken mince, onions, salt, black pepper, parsley eggs, panko, sesame oil and cilantro in the bowl.
5. Mix well.
6. Make small bite sized meatballs from the mixture.
7. Place the meatballs on the grill pan and grill them.
8. Dish out when they turn golden brown in color.
9. Your dish is ready to be served with BBQ sauce.

HONEY AND GARLIC CHICKEN STIR FRY

INGREDIENTS

- Two tablespoons of cornstarch
- One pound of chicken strips
- Two teaspoons of minced garlic
- Two tablespoons of vegetable oil
- Green onions for serving
- **For sauce:**
- One tablespoon of cornstarch
- A quarter cup of honey
- A quarter teaspoon of rice vinegar
- One teaspoon of red pepper flakes
- Half teaspoon of Shaoxing wine
- Two tablespoons of water

INSTRUCTIONS

1. Take a bowl.
2. Mix the Shaoxing wine, water, red pepper flakes, honey, and cornstarch to make sauce.
3. Keep aside.
4. Take a pan and add the vegetable oil into the pan.
5. Add the pork chops and stir fry the chicken strips in the oil until they turn crispy.
6. Add the garlic, sliced onion, and cornstarch into the pan.
7. Cook the ingredients well for fifteen minutes and add the sauce into the mixture.
8. Mix the ingredients well.
9. Add the green onions into the mixture.
10. Stir fry for five minutes and dish out.
11. Serve hot.

COOK TIME: 20 mins
SERVING: 4

MINCED PORK CONGEE

INGREDIENTS

- Half teaspoon of grated ginger
- Half pound of minced pork
- One teaspoon of Shaoxing wine
- Two teaspoons of minced garlic
- A quarter teaspoon of sugar
- One and a half teaspoon of soy sauce
- One tablespoon of cornstarch
- Six cups of water
- Two tablespoons of vegetable oil
- One cup of corn kernels
- Half cup of rice
- Chopped scallions for serving

COOK TIME: *30 mins*
SERVING: *4*

INSTRUCTIONS

1. Take a pan and add the vegetable oil into the pan.
2. Add the pork mince and stir fry the pork in the oil until it turns crispy.
3. Add the garlic, ginger, sugar, soy sauce, water, corn, rice, and cornstarch into the pan.
4. Cook the ingredients well for fifteen minutes and add the Shaoxing wine into the mixture.
5. Mix the ingredients well.
6. Add the chopped scallion on top and dish out.
7. Serve hot.

MISO AND MUSHROOM SOUP

INGREDIENTS

- Two packs of Chinese noodles
- Five cups of chicken stock
- One cup of shiitake mushrooms
- Two tablespoons of miso paste
- Four tablespoons of Shaoxing wine
- One tablespoon of soy sauce
- One tablespoon of oyster sauce
- Half cup of chopped green onions
- Two teaspoons of sesame oil
- Salt to taste

COOK TIME: 30 mins
SERVING: 2

INSTRUCTIONS

1. Take a sauce pan.
2. Add the sesame oil, and shiitake mushroom pieces into the pan.
3. Cook well for five to ten minutes and then add stock when they turn golden brown.
4. Add the miso paste, soy sauce, and oyster sauce into the pan.
5. Boil the mixture well.
6. Add the Shaoxing wine, mushrooms, salt and black pepper into the mixture.
7. Add the noodles into the mixture
8. Cook the ingredients until done and dish out into two bowls.
9. Add the spring onions on top.
10. Your dish is ready to be served.

PORK LO MEIN

INGREDIENTS

- Two tablespoons of cornstarch
- Two tablespoons of rice vinegar
- One pack of linguine noodles
- Two teaspoons of canola oil
- One teaspoon of sesame oil
- A quarter cup of soy sauce
- One teaspoon of sugar
- Half pound of pork tenderloins
- Two cups of snap peas
- One teaspoon of grated ginger
- One teaspoon of grated garlic
- One cup of chopped onions
- One cup of sliced mushrooms
- Green onions for serving

COOK TIME: 15 mins
SERVING: 4

INSTRUCTIONS

1. Take a bowl.
2. Mix the cornstarch, rice vinegar, sugar, soy sauce, and sesame oil to make sauce.
3. Keep aside.
4. Boil the noodles in a separate pan according to the instructions on the pack.
5. Dish out when the noodles are done.
6. Take a pan and add the vegetable oil into the pan.
7. Add the pork pieces and stir fry the pork in the oil until they turn crispy.
8. Dish out the pork when done.
9. Add the sliced mushrooms, grated ginger, grated garlic, snap peas and onions into the pan.
10. Cook the ingredients well for fifteen minutes and add the noodles, sauce and pork into the mixture.
11. Mix the ingredients well.
12. Add the green onions into the mixture.
13. Stir fry for five minutes and dish out.
14. Serve hot.

PAN FRIED BEEF NOODLES

INGREDIENTS

- Two packs of Chinese noodles
- One pound of beef strips
- A quarter cup of beef stock
- One cup of bok choy
- One cup of grated carrots
- One teaspoon of minced ginger
- One tablespoon of rice vinegar
- Two tablespoons of soy sauce
- A quarter teaspoon of sugar
- One sliced red chili
- Half cup of sliced scallions
- Two tablespoons of sesame oil
- Chopped green onions for garnishing

INSTRUCTIONS

1. Take a sauce pan.
2. Add the water into the pan.
3. Let the water boil and add the noodles into the water.
4. Boil the noodles for five to ten minutes and drain the excess water.
5. Take a wok.
6. Add the vegetable oil and scallions into the wok.
7. Cook the scallions well.
8. Add the ginger and sliced red chili into the wok.
9. Cook for two to three minutes.
10. Add the beef strips, carrots and bok choy into the pan.
11. Cook for ten minutes.
12. Add the beef stock, rice vinegar, soy sauce, and sugar into the pan.
13. Add the boiled noodles into the pan.
14. Cook the noodles in the sauce for five minutes.
15. Add the chopped green onions and sesame oil into the pan.
16. Mix well and dish out.
17. Your dish is ready to be served.

COOK TIME: 20 mins
SERVING: 4

PORK WITH PEKING SAUCE

INGREDIENTS

- Two teaspoons of dark soy sauce
- One teaspoon of cornstarch
- Half pound of pork strips
- One teaspoon of minced ginger
- Three tablespoons of bean sauce
- One teaspoon of kosher salt
- Four teaspoons of Chinese red wine
- One cup of red cabbage
- Three tablespoons of oil

COOK TIME: 5 mins
SERVING: 2

INSTRUCTIONS

1. Take a sauce pan.
2. Add the oil and pork pieces into the pan.
3. Cook well for five to ten minutes and then add stock when they turn golden brown.
4. Add the soy sauce, and bean sauce into the pan.
5. Cook the mixture well.
6. Add the cornstarch, ginger, salt and red wine into the mixture.
7. Add the red cabbage into the mixture.
8. Cook the ingredients until done and dish out into two bowls.
9. Your dish is ready to be served.

PORK AND ASPARAGUS STIR FRY

INGREDIENTS

- One tablespoon of oyster sauce
- Four cups of chicken stock
- Two cups of asparagus
- One pack of noodles
- Two teaspoons of grated ginger
- Two teaspoons of grated garlic
- Two teaspoons of sherry
- Two tablespoons of vegetable oil
- One cup of pork strips
- Two tablespoons of light soy sauce
- One cup of chopped green onions
- Black pepper to taste
- Salt to taste
- One teaspoon of sirarcha

COOK TIME: 30 mins
SERVING: 4

INSTRUCTIONS

1. Take a sauce pan.
2. Add the oil, garlic and ginger into the pan.
3. Cook for two to three minutes.
4. Add the asparagus and pork into the pan.
5. Cook well for five minutes and then add stock when they turn golden brown.
6. Add the light soy sauce, sirarcha, and oyster sauce into the pan.
7. Boil the mixture well.
8. Add the noodles, sherry, salt and black pepper into the mixture.
9. Cook the ingredients until done and dish out into four bowls.
10. Add the spring onions on top.
11. Your dish is ready to be served.

PORK RAMEN NOODLE SOUP

INGREDIENTS

- Two packs of ramen noodles
- Five cups of chicken broth
- Half cup of pork strips
- One cup of diced carrots
- One cup of shiitake mushrooms
- Four tablespoons of chili oil
- Two teaspoons of red chili pepper
- Four tablespoons of Shaoxing wine
- One tablespoon of soy sauce
- One tablespoon of oyster sauce
- Half cup of chopped green onions
- Two teaspoons of black pepper
- Two teaspoons of sesame oil
- Salt to taste

COOK TIME: 30 mins
SERVING: 2

INSTRUCTIONS

1. Take a sauce pan.
2. Add the sesame oil, and pork pieces into the pan.
3. Cook well for five to ten minutes and then add stock when they turn golden brown.
4. Add the soy sauce, red chili pepper, and oyster sauce into the pan.
5. Boil the mixture well.
6. Add the Shaoxing wine, mushrooms, carrots, salt and black pepper into the mixture.
7. Add the ramen noodles into the mixture
8. Cook the ingredients until done and dish out into two bowls.
9. Add the spring onions on top.
10. Your dish is ready to be served.

PORK AND MUSHROOM STIR FRY

INGREDIENTS

- A quarter cup of soy sauce
- A pound of pork strips
- Two teaspoons of grated garlic
- Two teaspoons of grated ginger
- Two teaspoons of cooking wine
- Two tablespoons of vegetable oil
- One teaspoon of oyster sauce
- Half pound of mushroom slices
- Two tablespoons of cornstarch
- One cup of sliced scallions
- White pepper to taste
- Salt to taste
- four teaspoons of water
- Cooked rice for serving

COOK TIME: 30 mins
SERVING: 4

INSTRUCTIONS

1. Take a mixing bowl.
2. Add the oyster sauce, pork strips, ginger, soy sauce, garlic, cornstarch, cooking wine, and the salt into the bowl.
3. Mix well and place it aside.
4. Take a large pan.
5. Add the oil into the pan and heat it well.
6. Add the scallions into the pan.
7. Cook well and then add the mushrooms, white pepper, salt and water.
8. Cook until the mushrooms are done.
9. Dish out when done.
10. Add the pork strips into the pan.
11. Cook the pork until it begins to turn white.
12. Toss the mushrooms back into the pan.
13. Mix well and cook for five minutes.
14. Add the stir-fry on a serving platter and serve with cooked rice.

Tip: You can use pork butt strips for extra juicy result in this stir fry recipe.

PINEAPPLE CHICKEN

INGREDIENTS

- Two tablespoons of cornstarch
- Two tablespoons of hoisin sauce
- One cup of bell pepper
- Two teaspoons of vegetable oil
- One teaspoon of brown sugar
- A quarter cup of soy sauce
- A quarter cup of pineapple juice
- A quarter cup of chicken broth
- One teaspoon of sugar
- Half pound of chicken strips
- Two cups of pineapple pieces
- One teaspoon of grated ginger
- One teaspoon of grated garlic
- Sesame seeds for serving

COOK TIME: 15 mins
SERVING: 4

INSTRUCTIONS

1. Take a bowl.
2. Mix the cornstarch, hoisin sauce, brown sugar, soy sauce, and pineapple juice to make sauce.
3. Keep aside.
4. Take a pan and add the vegetable oil into the pan.
5. Add the chicken pieces and stir fry the chicken in the oil until they turn crispy.
6. Dish out the chicken when done.
7. Add the pineapple pieces, grated ginger, grated garlic, and bell pepper into the pan.
8. Cook the ingredients well for fifteen minutes and add the sauce and chicken into the mixture.
9. Mix the ingredients well.
10. Add the sesame seeds into the mixture.
11. Stir fry for five minutes and dish out.
12. Your dish is ready to be served.

QUICK LAMB WITH SCALLIONS

INGREDIENTS

- One tablespoon of canola oil
- Two tablespoons of soy sauce
- One tablespoon of brown sugar
- One tablespoon of Sichuan peppers
- One cup of sliced scallions
- Two cups of lamb mince
- Two tablespoons of cumin powder
- Half teaspoon of minced garlic
- Two tablespoons of lime juice
- Salt to taste
- Black pepper
- Half cup of green onions
- A quarter cup of freshly chopped cilantro
- Two tablespoons of soy sauce

INSTRUCTIONS

1. Take a large pan.
2. Add the scallions, garlic and canola oil into the pan.
3. Add the lamb mince when the garlic turns golden brown.
4. Cook well.
5. Add the salt, black pepper, soy sauce, lime juice, brown sugar, Sichuan pepper, and cumin powder into the pan.
6. Cook the ingredients for fifteen to twenty minutes.
7. Dish out when done.
8. Garnish the dish with chopped cilantro and green onions.
9. Your dish is ready to be served.

COOK TIME: *20 mins*
SERVING: *2*

RICE PUDDING

INGREDIENTS

- Five cups of milk
- Half teaspoon of salt
- One teaspoon of vanilla extract
- A quarter cup of sugar
- One cup of soaked rice
- Half teaspoon of cinnamon powder

COOK TIME: 30 mins
SERVING: 4

INSTRUCTIONS

1. Take a pan.
2. Add the rice, sugar, salt, milk and vanilla extract into the bowl.
3. Cook the ingredients well for thirty minutes and then dish out into a serving bowl.
4. Garnish the dish with cinnamon powder.
5. Your dish is ready to be served.

SWEET AND SOUR VEGETABLE BAO BUNS

INGREDIENTS

- Four bao buns
- A pound of mixed vegetables
- One tablespoon of soy sauce
- A quarter teaspoon of white pepper powder
- One tablespoon of rice wine
- Two teaspoons of corn starch
- Salt to taste
- One cup of chili pepper
- One teaspoon of minced ginger
- One teaspoon of minced garlic
- Two tablespoons of vegetable oil
- One tablespoon of sugar
- Sweet and sour sauce
- Three tablespoons of chopped green onions
- Sesame seeds for serving

INSTRUCTIONS

1. Take a bowl.
2. Add the vegetables, rice wine, white pepper powder, soy sauce, cornstarch and salt into the bowl.
3. Mix well.
4. Take a pan.
5. Add the vegetable oil into it.
6. Add the vegetables in the pan and cook them well.
7. Add the sugar, chili pepper, garlic, ginger, salt and black pepper on top of the pork pieces.
8. Dish out the vegetables when done.
9. Cut the bao buns in between to make a pocket and add the cooked mixture into it.
10. Pour the sweet and sour sauce on top of the vegetables.
11. Garnish the dish with green onions and sesame seeds.
12. Your dish is ready to be served.

COOK TIME: *17 mins*
SERVING: *4*

SESAME COOKIES

INGREDIENTS

- One whole egg
- One and a half cup of all-purpose flour
- A pinch of kosher salt
- One cup of unsalted butter
- Half cup of brown sugar
- One cup of sugar
- Half teaspoon of baking soda
- One teaspoon of almond extract
- Sesame seeds for coating

COOK TIME: 15 mins
SERVING: 60

INSTRUCTIONS

1. Preheat the oven to 220 degrees.
2. Take a bowl.
3. Add the eggs and almond extract into the bowl.
4. Mix the ingredients well until the mixture turns fluffy.
5. Add the butter, baking soda sugar, salt and all-purpose flour into the bowl.
6. Mix the ingredients well.
7. Knead the dough and roll it out into a semi thick sheet.
8. Cut round cookies out of the dough using a cutter and cover it with the sesame seeds.
9. Take a baking tray.
10. Grease the tray well and add the cookies on the baking tray.
11. Make sure you flatten the cookie batter and then place it in the oven.
12. Bake the cookies for fifteen minutes or until light golden brown in color.
13. Dish out when done.
14. Your dish is ready to be served.

SHRIMP WITH GARLIC NOODLES

INGREDIENTS

- Half teaspoon of grated garlic
- One tablespoon of tahini
- A quarter teaspoon of dark soy sauce
- Two teaspoons of light soy sauce
- Two packs of boiled egg noodles
- Salt to taste
- Black pepper to taste
- One tablespoon of Chinese black vinegar
- One tablespoon of sesame seeds
- Cilantro for serving
- Three tablespoons of vegetable oil
- Half pound of roasted shrimps

COOK TIME: 30 mins
SERVING: 4

INSTRUCTIONS

1. Take a pan.
2. Add the vegetable oil into the pan.
3. Add the garlic into the pan.
4. Cook the garlic until it turns golden brown in color.
5. Add the dark soy sauce, light soy sauce, Chinese black vinegar, tahini, salt, and black pepper into the pan.
6. Add the boiled noodles into the pan.
7. Mix everything well to make sure the sauces reach all the noodles.
8. Cook for five to ten minutes.
9. Add the sesame seeds, cilantro and shrimps into the pan.
10. Mix well and dish out.
11. Your dish is ready to be served.

STEAMED PORK WITH VEGETABLES

INGREDIENTS

- Two cups of chopped preserved vegetables
- One teaspoon of Shaoxing wine
- A quarter cup of soy sauce
- One tablespoon of white pepper
- Two cups of pork mince
- Two teaspoons of cornstarch
- Half teaspoon of sugar
- Half cup of chopped scallions
- A quarter teaspoon of sesame oil

COOK TIME: 20 mins
SERVING: 4

INSTRUCTIONS

1. Take a mixing bowl.
2. Add the wine, vegetables, soy sauce, pork, white pepper, cornstarch, sugar, scallions and sesame oil into the bowl.
3. Mix the ingredients well.
4. Take a steamer and add water into it.
5. Let the steamer get ready and you make small thin patties using the mixture.
6. Place the patties in the steamer and close the lid.
7. Dish out the patties after thirty minutes.
8. Your dish is ready to be served.

STICKY PORK BAO BUNS

INGREDIENTS

- Four bao buns
- Four tablespoons of vegetable oil
- Half tablespoon of minced garlic
- Half tablespoon of minced ginger
- One cup of chopped onions
- One tablespoon of light muscavado sugar
- Salt to taste
- Black pepper to taste
- Half teaspoon of turmeric powder
- Half teaspoon of fennel seeds
- One tablespoon of coriander powder
- Three curry leaves
- Three tablespoons of Shaoxing wine
- One pound of diced pork
- Chopped green onions for serving

INSTRUCTIONS

1. Take a pan.
2. Add the vegetable oil into it.
3. Add the chopped onions into the pan.
4. Cook well until they turn soft.
5. Add the garlic and ginger into the pan.
6. Add the pork pieces into it and cook them until they turn golden brown.
7. Add turmeric powder, muscavado sugar, curry leaves, coriander powder, fennel seeds, salt, Shaoxing wine and black pepper into the bowl.
8. Coat the pork pieces with the mixture.
9. Dish out when done.
10. Cut the bao buns in between to make a pocket and add the cooked mixture into it.
11. Pour the sweet and sour sauce on top of the pork.
12. Garnish the dish with chopped green onions.
13. Your dish is ready to be served.

COOK TIME: 30 mins
SERVING: 4

STEAMED PORK WITH RICE POWDER

INGREDIENTS

- Two tablespoons of rice powder
- One pound of pork cubes
- One teaspoon of baking soda
- Two teaspoons of soy sauce
- One teaspoon of Shaoxing wine
- **For sauce:**
- A quarter cup of water
- Half cup of oyster sauce
- Half cup of soy sauce
- One teaspoon of grated ginger
- A quarter teaspoon of rice vinegar
- One teaspoon of red pepper flakes
- Half teaspoon of Shaoxing wine

COOK TIME: 20 mins
SERVING: 4

INSTRUCTIONS

1. Take a bowl.
2. Mix the Shaoxing wine, water, grated ginger, red pepper flakes, oyster sauce, and soy sauce to make sauce.
3. Keep aside.
4. Take a bowl.
5. Add the rice powder, pork pieces, baking soda, soy sauce and Shaoxing wine into the bowl.
6. Mix well.
7. Take a steamer and add water into it.
8. Let the steamer get ready.
9. Place the pork pieces in the steamer and close the lid.
10. Dish out the pieces after thirty minutes.
11. Your dish is ready to be served with the prepared sauce.

STICKY CHINESE PORK

INGREDIENTS

- A quarter cup of honey
- Half cup of mangetout
- Three pounds of pork pieces
- Salt to taste
- Two tablespoons of canola oil
- Black pepper to taste
- Three tablespoons of cornstarch
- Two tablespoons of minced ginger
- Two tablespoons of minced garlic
- Half cup of chicken broth
- A quarter cup of soy sauce
- Half cup of mixed vegetables
- Half teaspoon of Chinese five spice powder

COOK TIME: 25 mins
SERVING: 4

INSTRUCTIONS

1. Take a sauce pan.
2. Add the oil into the sauce pan.
3. Add the pork pieces into the pan.
4. Season them with salt and black pepper.
5. Cook well and dish out.
6. Add the garlic, ginger, chicken broth, Chinese five spice powder, mixed vegetables, honey, ketchup, soy sauce, mangetout and cornstarch into the pan.
7. Mix well and let it thicken into a sauce.
8. Add the pork pieces into the saucy mixture.
9. Cook for ten minutes and dish out.
10. Your dish is ready to be served.

STEWED LAMB WITH RADISH

INGREDIENTS

- One cup of diced daikon radish
- Two tablespoons of vegetable oil
- One cup of chopped cabbage
- Salt to taste
- Half teaspoon of grated ginger
- Half teaspoon of grated garlic
- Two tablespoons of soy sauce
- Half cup of chopped onions
- Two tablespoons of lime juice
- One pound of lamb pieces
- One cup of chopped tomatoes

COOK TIME: 35 mins
SERVING: 2

INSTRUCTIONS

1. Heat the oil in a pot.
2. Add the onion into the pot.
3. Cook and stir for three minutes, or until the onion is tender.
4. Add the tomatoes in the pot and stir fry.
5. Add the lamb and vegetables into the pot.
6. Add the stock, daikon radish, soy sauce, brown sugar, garlic, and ginger into the pot.
7. Dish out the broth.
8. Add the lime juice on top.
9. Your dish is ready to be served.

STEWED LAMB IN BROWN SAUCE

INGREDIENTS

- One tablespoon of brown sugar
- Three tablespoons of red bean curd
- A quarter cup of chee hou sauce
- Two tablespoons of vegetable oil
- Two tablespoons of soy sauce
- A quarter cup of tangerine peel
- Half cup of chopped onions
- Two tablespoons of lime juice
- A quarter cup of chili sauce
- One pound of lamb pieces
- Black pepper to taste
- Half cup of red bell pepper
- Half cup of oyster sauce
- Half teaspoon of grated ginger
- Half teaspoon of grated garlic

COOK TIME: 15 mins
SERVING: 2

INSTRUCTIONS

1. Heat the oil in a stockpot over medium-high heat for the broth.
2. Add the onion into the pot.
3. Cook and stir for three minutes, or until the onion is tender.
4. Add the lamb and vegetables into the pot.
5. Add the stock, chee hou sauce, oyster sauce, soy sauce, brown sugar, garlic, and ginger into the pot.
6. Reduce the heat to low, cover, and leave to simmer for twenty minutes.
7. Just before serving, add the lime juice to the stew.
8. Dish out the stew.
9. Your dish is ready to be served.

STWED NOODLES WITH LAMB

INGREDIENTS

- A pinch of saffron threads
- Half cup of golden raisins
- Two tablespoons of peanut oil
- A quarter cup of soy sauce
- Half cup of chopped onions
- One Star Anise
- One teaspoon of dried lemongrass
- Green onions for garnishing
- Three pack of vermicelli noodles
- One pound of lamb shanks
- Four cups of chicken stock
- One cup of chopped almonds
- Half teaspoon of grated ginger
- Half teaspoon of grated garlic

COOK TIME: 50 mins
SERVING: 6

INSTRUCTIONS

1. Heat the oil in a pot over medium-high.
2. Add the onion into the pot.
3. Cook and stir for three minutes, or until the onion is tender.
4. Add the garlic and ginger into the pot,
5. Add the lamb shanks and almonds into the pot.
6. Saute the ingredients well.
7. Add the stock, soy sauce, star anise, saffron, lemongrass, golden raisins, and noodles into the pot.
8. Reduce the heat to low, cover, and leave to simmer for twenty minutes.
9. Dish out the stew and add the green onions on top.
10. Your dish is ready to be served.

STIR FRIED RIBS WITH STINKY TOFU

INGREDIENTS

- Two tablespoons of crushed garlic
- One teaspoon of Sichuan pepper
- Two cups of tofu pieces
- Half pound of ribs
- Two tablespoons of sesame oil
- Two tablespoons of oyster sauce
- Two tablespoons of soy sauce
- Three tablespoons of chili oil
- One tablespoon of sugar
- Salt to taste
- Black pepper to taste
- Two tablespoons of cornstarch

COOK TIME: 20 mins
SERVING: 2

INSTRUCTIONS

1. Take a bowl.
2. Add the cornstarch, tofu cubes, salt and black pepper in the bowl.
3. Take a pan.
4. Add the sesame oil into the pan.
5. Add the tofu pieces and cook them for five minutes.
6. Add the ribs into the mixture.
7. Take a bowl.
8. Add the crushed garlic, Sichuan pepper, oyster sauce, chili oil, soy sauce, and sugar into the bowl.
9. Mix the ingredients well.
10. Pour the sauce into the pan and cook well.
11. Dish out when done.
12. Your dish is ready to be served.

SPICY CHILI GARLIC SHRIMP

INGREDIENTS

- A pound of shrimps
- One tablespoon of soy sauce
- A quarter teaspoon of white pepper powder
- One tablespoon of rice wine
- Two teaspoons of corn starch
- Salt to taste
- One tablespoon of red pepper flakes
- One teaspoon of minced ginger
- One teaspoon of minced garlic
- Two tablespoons of vegetable oil
- One tablespoon of sirarcha
- Sesame seeds for serving
- Dried chilies for serving

COOK TIME: *17 mins*
SERVING: *4*

INSTRUCTIONS

1. Take a bowl.
2. Add the shrimp pieces, rice wine, white pepper powder, soy sauce, cornstarch and salt into the bowl.
3. Mix well.
4. Take a pan.
5. Add the vegetable oil into it.
6. Add the shrimp pieces in the pan and cook them well.
7. Add the sirarcha, red pepper flakes, garlic, ginger, salt and black pepper on top of the shrimp pieces.
8. Dish out the shrimp pieces when done and place them on the serving dish.
9. Garnish the dish with dried chilies and sesame seeds.
10. Your dish is ready to be served.

SPICY BOILED FISH

INGREDIENTS

- Half teaspoon of Sichuan chili bean paste
- Half teaspoon of chili powder
- Three cups of fish broth
- Three tablespoons of Shaoxing wine
- One pound of diced fish pieces
- Chopped green onions for serving
- Four tablespoons of vegetable oil
- Half tablespoon of minced garlic
- Half tablespoon of minced ginger
- One cup of chopped onions
- One tablespoon of light soy sauce
- Salt to taste
- Black pepper to taste

INSTRUCTIONS

1. Take a pan.
2. Add the vegetable oil into it.
3. Add the chopped onions into the pan.
4. Cook well until they turn soft.
5. Add the garlic and ginger into the pan.
6. Add the fish pieces into it and cook them until they turn golden brown.
7. Add Sichuan chili bean paste, soy sauce, chili powder, fish broth, salt, Shaoxing wine and black pepper into the bowl.
8. Boil the ingredients for twenty minutes.
9. Dish out when done.
10. Garnish the dish with chopped green onions.
11. Your dish is ready to be served.

COOK TIME: 30 mins
SERVING: 4

SPICY STIR FRIED RICE CAKES

INGREDIENTS

- Half teaspoon of grated garlic
- A quarter cup of jalapeno pepper
- Half cup of chopped Thai bird chilies
- A quarter teaspoon of spicy bean paste
- Two teaspoons of light soy sauce
- Two cups of rice cakes
- Half pound of pork belly
- Salt to taste
- Black pepper to taste
- One tablespoon of rice vinegar
- One cup of chopped scallions
- One tablespoon of sesame seeds
- Green onions for serving
- Three tablespoons of vegetable oil

INSTRUCTIONS

1. Take a pan.
2. Add the vegetable oil and scallions into the pan.
3. Cook the scallions well.
4. Add the garlic into the pan.
5. Cook the garlic until it turns golden brown in color.
6. Add the pork belly, jalapeno peppers, Thai bird chilies into the mixture.
7. Add the spicy bean paste, light soy sauce, rice vinegar, salt, and black pepper into the pan.
8. Add the rice cakes into the ingredients.
9. Cook for five to ten minutes.
10. Add the sesame seeds, and green onions into the pan.
11. Mix well and dish out.
12. Your dish is ready to be served.

COOK TIME: 20 mins
SERVING: 4

SPICY CUMIN LAMB

INGREDIENTS

- One tablespoon of rice vinegar
- One teaspoon of salt
- Two teaspoons of cornstarch
- Half teaspoon of black pepper
- Three tablespoons of vegetable oil
- One pound of lamb strips
- Two tablespoons of cumin seeds
- One cup of scallion slices
- Two tablespoons of red flakes
- Two tablespoons of soy sauce
- Two tablespoons of minced garlic
- Two tablespoons of minced ginger
- Two lime wedges
- Chopped cilantro for serving

COOK TIME: *30 mins*
SERVING: *2*

INSTRUCTIONS

1. Take a sauce pan.
2. Add vegetable oil, ginger and garlic into the pan.
3. Cook the ingredients for two to three minutes and add the lamb strips into the pan.
4. Cook the lamb strips for ten to fifteen minutes.
5. Add the soy sauce, rice vinegar, salt, cornstarch, black pepper, red pepper flakes, scallions and cumin seeds into the pan.
6. Mix the mixture well.
7. Cook the ingredients until done and dish out into a serving dish.
8. Add the chopped cilantro and lime wedges on top.
9. Your dish is ready to be served.

SPICY GARLIC BEEF

INGREDIENTS

- Half teaspoon of grated garlic
- One tablespoon of red pepper flakes
- A quarter teaspoon of dark soy sauce
- Two teaspoons of light soy sauce
- Salt to taste
- Black pepper to taste
- One tablespoon of sesame seeds
- Cilantro for serving
- Three tablespoons of vegetable oil
- Half pound of beef strips

COOK TIME: 20 mins
SERVING: 4

INSTRUCTIONS

1. Take a pan.
2. Add the vegetable oil into the pan.
3. Add the garlic and beef into the pan.
4. Cook the garlic until it turns golden brown in color.
5. Add the dark soy sauce, light soy sauce, red pepper flakes, salt, and black pepper into the pan.
6. Cook for five to ten minutes.
7. Add the sesame seeds, and cilantro into the pan.
8. Mix well and dish out.
9. Your dish is ready to be served.

TOFU STIR FRY WITH CASHEWS

INGREDIENTS

- A quarter cup of water
- One cup of raw cashews
- Four tablespoons of hoisin sauce
- One tablespoon of soy sauce
- A pound of tofu cubes
- Two teaspoons of grated garlic
- Two teaspoons of rice vinegar
- Two tablespoons of vegetable oil
- Two tablespoons of cornstarch
- One cup of sliced scallions
- Black pepper to taste
- Salt to taste
- One teaspoon of water
- Cooked rice for serving

COOK TIME: 30 mins
SERVING: 4

INSTRUCTIONS

1. Take a mixing bowl.
2. Add the tofu cubes, ginger, soy sauce, garlic, hoisin sauce, and the salt into the bowl.
3. Mix well and place them aside.
4. Take a large pan.
5. Add the oil into the pan and heat it well.
6. Add the cashews into the pan.
7. Cook well and roast them for three to five minutes.
8. Dish out when done.
9. Add the tofu cubes into the pan.
10. Toss the cashew back into the pan.
11. Add water and cornstarch into the pan.
12. Mix well and cook for five minutes.
13. Dish out and serve with cooked rice.

TOMATO AND EGG STIR FRY

INGREDIENTS

- One tablespoon of rice vinegar
- One teaspoon of salt
- Two teaspoons of oyster sauce
- One teaspoon of cooking wine
- Half teaspoon of black pepper
- Three tablespoons of vegetable oil
- Four whole eggs
- Two cup of chopped tomatoes
- Two tablespoons of soy sauce
- Two tablespoons of minced garlic
- Two tablespoons of minced ginger
- Chopped cilantro for serving

COOK TIME: 30 mins
SERVING: 2

INSTRUCTIONS

1. Take a sauce pan.
2. Add vegetable oil, ginger and garlic into the pan.
3. Cook the ingredients for two to three minutes and add the egg one by one into the pan.
4. Cook the eggs by continuously mixing them for ten to fifteen minutes.
5. Add the oyster sauce, soy sauce, rice vinegar, salt, cooking wine, black pepper, and tomatoes into the pan.
6. Mix the mixture well.
7. Cook the ingredients until done and dish out into a serving dish.
8. Add the chopped cilantro on top.
9. Your dish is ready to be served.

VEGETABLE CHINESE SALAD

INGREDIENTS

- Two cups of baked tofu pieces
- Two cup of chopped celery stalks
- Half cup of chopped turnips
- Half cup of shredded carrots
- Half cup of shredded cucumber
- Two cups of lettuce
- Half cup of chopped green onions
- Half cup of roasted cashews
- **For dressing:**
- Two tablespoons of sugar
- A quarter cup of soy sauce
- Two tablespoons of rice vinegar
- Salt to taste
- Two tablespoons of sesame oil

INSTRUCTIONS

1. Add the baked tofu pieces, celery stalks, turnips, carrots, lettuce, shredded cucumber and roasted cashews into the large bowl.
2. Take a bowl.
3. Add the salt, rice vinegar, sesame oil, soy sauce, and sugar into the bowl.
4. Mix the ingredients well.
5. Drizzle the prepared dressing on top of the salad mixture.
6. Toss the mixture and add into a serving dish.
7. Your dish is ready to be served.

COOK TIME: *20 mins*
SERVING: *2*

WONTON AND NOODLE SOUP

INGREDIENTS

- One cup of all-purpose flour
- Half cup of water
- Two tablespoons of Sichuan pepper
- A quarter cup of chopped scallions
- One cup of minced pork
- One cup of minced beef
- Two teaspoons of shaoxing wine
- Half cup of stock
- One teaspoon of garlic powder
- One teaspoon of ginger powder
- One teaspoon of sesame oil
- Salt to taste
- Black pepper
- **For Soup:**
- One pack of Chinese noodles
- Half teaspoon of sesame oil
- One teaspoon of soy sauce
- Four cups of any stock
- Black pepper to taste
- Salt to taste
- Two tablespoons of Chinese cinnamon
- Spring onion for serving
- Toasted sesame seeds for serving

COOK TIME: 20 mins
SERVING: 4

INSTRUCTIONS

1. Take a large bowl.
2. Add the flour, salt and water in a bowl.
3. Mix the dough and knead the ingredients well.
4. Take a pan.
5. Add the oil, scallions, pork mince, beef mince, Sichuan peppers, stock, shaoxing wine, ginger powder, garlic powder, black pepper, and salt into the pan.
6. Cook the mixture well until the ingredients are done.
7. Roll out the dough into a thin sheet.
8. Cut small round circles in the dough.
9. Add the meat filling in the circle and shape it out in the form of a wonton.
10. Take a large saucepan.
11. Add the ingredients of the soup and let them boil for two minutes.
12. Add the wontons into the pan.
13. Cook the soup well until the wontons are done.
14. Garnish the soup with spring onion and sesame seeds.
15. Your dish is ready to be served.

ZUCCHINI AND SHRIMP STIR FRY

INGREDIENTS

- Three tablespoons of soy sauce
- One pound of shrimp pieces
- Two cups of cabbage
- One teaspoon of minced garlic
- One cup of grated carrots
- One cup zucchini pieces
- Half cup of sliced onions
- Two tablespoons of vegetable oil
- Sesame seeds for garnishing

COOK TIME: 30 mins
SERVING: 4

INSTRUCTIONS

1. Take a pan and add the vegetable oil into the pan.
2. Add the garlic, and onion into the pan.
3. Cook the onion for five minutes.
4. Add soy sauce, zucchini pieces, shrimp pieces, and carrots into the pan.
5. Mix the ingredients well.
6. Cook the ingredients well for fifteen minutes.
7. Add the sesame seeds into the mixture.
8. Stir fry for five minutes and dish out.
9. Serve hot.

Conclusion

Chinese are great at using what the nature gives them. Chinese likewise really like to talk while eating. They utilize the eating time to speak with one another with regards to their life, work, study, and so on. In the west, individuals might make an arrangement for some espresso to discuss something, while in China, it is usually a dinner.

This cookbook incorporates authentic recipes including vegan recipes bao bun recipes, soup recipes, lamb recipes, beef recipes, stir fry recipes, dumpling recipes, and so much more. So, start cooking today with this delicious Chinese cookbook!

CHINESE

COOKBOOK

70 Easy Recipes for Traditional Food
from China

Maki Blanc

Introduction

Chinese cuisine (Chinese meals) developed in various parts of Asia and has spread to many other countries. Geographic differences in culture vary widely between China's various regions, resulting in various food styles. There are eight major regional types of food in the United States. In Chinese culture, a meal usually consists of two or more basic elements: the first is a complex carbohydrate or flour, referred to as a staple meal in Chinese, and the second is corresponding dishes of veggies, meat, seafood, or other ingredients.

Most Chinese cuisine relies heavily on rice. On the other hand, Northern China is dominated by wheat-based items such as pasta and steamed bread, while southern China is dominated by rice. In Traditional Chinese, chopsticks are the main feeding utensil for real food, while a large, plain spoon is used for sauces and other fluids. Veganism is not unusual or rare in China, but it is only practiced by a small percentage of the population, as it does in the West.

Many Chinese foods, whether hot or moderate, share a similar base. "The holy trinity of Chinese cuisine is ginger, garlic, and chili. The wok is the core of Chinese cooking and is needed for any stir-fry. There is hardly any limit on the number of traditional meals that can fall out of an unpretentious wok on the cooktop: ginger meat, sticky rice, meat chow fun. The speedy method can preserve nutrients in the veggies while also reducing fuel consumption.

Chinese cuisine is one of the most well-known cooking methods, with a long history and a place among the Chinese cultural resources. It is well-known all over the globe. Chinese cuisine's arrival of Chinese food has evolved over centuries, creating a rich cultural knowledge characterized by a fine selection of ingredients, precise preparation, careful attention to the level of heat, and substantial nourishment.

The evolution and diversity of Chinese cuisine are also a result of China's long history. With each generation, new techniques were made until the craft of food preparation reached its height.

"Chinese Cookbook" is a complete recipe book based on all types of Chinese dishes. It has four chapters with detailed knowledge of the introduction to Chinese cuisine. Recipes from different regions of China are given in each chapter. These chapters are characterized into breakfast, appetizers, snacks, lunch, dinner, desserts, soups, salad, and India's most famous dishes. Try these dishes at your home and make your meals more like Chinese.

Chapter 1: Introduction to Chinese Cuisine

China has a four-thousand-year background, and the People in China have developed a vibrant culture, of which Chinese cuisine is an integral part. The majority of foreign tourists to China are blown away by the country's cuisine. Color, aroma, and taste are all important aspects of Chinese food. Chinese chefs strive to coordinate the colors of their dishes to make them appear more attractive. Some meals are simple, while others are vibrant. A table of Chinese cuisine tends to be very bright and appealing.

The manner Chinese food tastes is extremely significant. Chefs use spices, as well as the components in a recipe, to make food smell healthy. Taste, on the other hand, is the most distinctive attribute of Chinese cuisine. Various methods are used to make Chinese food tasty, providing a great deal of gratification to the palate. Chinese cuisine offers a wide range of material options, which helps Chinese chefs to be more inventive. These involve a variety of grains, fruits, and meat from various animals. The most popular cooking technique is stir-frying. There are eight major divisions of Chinese cuisine. The quality and artistic elegance of Chinese dishes are emphasized in all eight branches.

1.1 History of Chinese Cuisine

Food and its processing have advanced to the point that it is considered an art form in China. People in China, regardless of income, find tasty and healthy meals to be a basic requirement. "Food is the first need of the citizens," says an old Chinese proverb.

Over centuries, this craft has been developed and perfected. According to history, Chinese cuisine first appeared in the 15th century BC during the Shang dynasty but was adopted by Yi Yin, the first Party Leader. Both of China's prevailing ideologies had profound effects on the country's macroeconomic background, but it is less well established that they have shaped the creative arts' growth.

The cultural and intellectual aspects of cooking and eating were significant to Confucius. According to the Chinese, it is considered common manners to bring guests to your home while having enough food. Confucius developed cooking and dinner etiquette codes, the majority of which have survived to this day. The most noticeable instance is slicing bite-sized chunks of meat and veggies during the kitchen's food manufacturing process instead of using a blade at dinner, which is found impolite.

Instead of sampling the different pieces, Confucius advocated combining ingredients and flavorings to create a cohesive dish. His main concern was maintaining harmony. He claimed and demonstrated that there could be no flavor without a combination of ingredients. He also stressed the importance of dish appearance, including color, form, and design. Most notably, preparing became an art rather than a chore, and he was a follower of the concept of "survive to eat" instead of "eat to survive."

On the other side, Tao was a proponent of studies into the nutritional aspects of food and cooking. Taoists were much more concerned with the life-giving kinds of proteins than with their flavor.

For centuries, the Chinese have known that all kinds of roots, herbs, fungi, and crops have medicinal properties. They have told the world that undercooking kills the nutritious value of food, and they have discovered that foods with a good taste also have therapeutic benefits.

1.2 History of Traditional Dishes of Chinese Food

Chinese cuisine has a long tradition, dating back to around 5000 BC. Over such a long period of time, the Chinese have established their distinct method of food preparation. Their methods for recognizing materials to produce optimal blends, multi-phased preparation strategies, and multi-phased flavoring administration have evolved. The ancient Chinese eat a very balanced diet, and we can deduct from historical evidence that agriculture in China began about 5,000 years ago.

Chinese cuisine is known for its diversity and adaptability. Food has been at the center of social communication since prehistoric times, and many modern meals, with their varied aromas and tastes, can be linked back to ancient Chinese food practices. Food has often been regarded as an art form in China, emphasizing the preparation and presentation of food. Although there were few veggies in ancient China, they were an important part of food types. They consumed veggies with their staple meal, rice, since they could manage it. China is known as one of the world's largest first wine-producing nations. Wine has been endowed with historical and emotional meaning since its creation, representing political and social life and artistic ideas.

Pork, along with other meats such as meat, lamb, duck, chicken, pigeon, and others, is the most popular in China. Pork, which was indigenous to China, was consumed by the Chinese people as early as 4000 or 3000 BC. Tea consumption is regarded as an elegant art form in China, with numerous customs and traditions. Noodles are another traditional Chinese dish. Noodles have a long tradition dating back to the Eastern Han Dynasty.

Agricultural production appears to have played a significant role in China's history, with ancient agricultural activities playing a key role in the country's political, financial, cultural, and ideological advancements.

1.3 Nutritional Information and Benefits of Chinese Food

Chinese food is not only nutrient-dense, but it is also well-balanced, providing all the body and bloodstream need to stay in good shape. The Chinese claim that a significant proportion of veggies and a tiny slice of meat can be fairly designed. Meat is important because it adds refined carbs to the diet. Chinese foods are low in fat, refined carbohydrates, and cholesterol, enabling our bodies to know when they are full. This encourages people who eat Chinese food to consume a more acceptable amount of food and avoid overdoing it on calories. Chinese cuisine also helps to regulate food consumption by emphasizing liquid foods.

According to the yin (cooling wet and moist products) and Yang (heat-producing foods) concepts, all Chinese meals are produced. Almost every dish in Chinese cuisine is prepared with a balance of yin and yang components. Carbohydrates are yin, whereas protein-rich foods are yang. Tea, in general, is well-known for its beneficial effects in treating cardiovascular disease, metabolism, and cancer risk. Chinese chefs haven't forgotten the ancient belief that such ingredients have healing uses.

1.4 Key Ingredients of Chinese Food

Traditional Chinese cuisine achieves its iconic status by creating the perfect balance of spicy, sour, salty, and savory flavors, so you face the risk of disrupting this fine balance by replacing core ingredients. Here is a list of key ingredients used in Chinese cuisine.

- Dried chilies
- Fermented black beans
- White rice vinegar
- Shaoxing rice wine
- Light soy sauce
- Chinese five-spice
- Chili bean sauce
- Dark soy sauce
- Sichuan peppercorns
- Sesame oil
- Dried mushrooms
- Oyster sauce

Chapter 2: Chinese Appetizers Recipes

PAN FRIED VEGETABLE DUMPLINGS

INGREDIENTS

For the Filling
- 24 packaged dumpling skins
- 1 tablespoon vegetable oil
- ¼ teaspoon salt
- 2 teaspoons cornstarch
- ½ cup carrot
- 2 teaspoons soy sauce
- ½ teaspoon pepper powder
- ½ teaspoon sugar
- 2 teaspoons sesame oil
- ½ cup five-spice tofu
- 2 tablespoons minced garlic
- 1 tablespoon scallion whites
- ½ cup seitan
- 1 cup cabbage
- ¼ ounce ear mushrooms

For the Dipping Sauce
- 2 teaspoons rice vinegar
- 1 scallion, sliced

COOK TIME: 60 mins
SERVING: 24
- 1 teaspoon sesame oil

INSTRUCTIONS

1. In a big mixing bowl, mix carrots, cabbage, seitan, mushrooms, broccoli, garlic, spring onion, salt, soy sauce, sesame oil, red pepper, salt, and cornflour.
2. Place a little less than a teaspoon of the fill in the wrap's core to begin sealing the dumpling.
3. Pinch the middle of the wrapper together after folding it in half.
4. In a large nonstick baking pan, add the remaining tablespoon of oil on medium heat to griddle the dumplings.
5. Whenever the oil is glinting, add the dumplings and pan-fry until golden brown on the bottom.
6. In a small cup, mix soy sauce, sesame oil, mustard, and spring onion. Serve warm with dumplings.

SHREDDED CHICKEN SALAD WITH GOCHUJANG DRESSING

INGREDIENTS

For the Salad
- ¼ English cucumber
- ¼ small red onion
- ½ bunch watercress
- 3 ounces leaf lettuce
- 2 cups water
- 1 tablespoon table salt
- 1 whole chicken breast half
- 1 cup sake
- 3 slices of ginger

For the Dressing
- 4 teaspoons gochujang
- 2 teaspoons rice vinegar
- 2 tablespoons mirin
- 2 tablespoons sesame oil

COOK TIME: 30 mins
SERVING: 4

INSTRUCTIONS

21. Combine the salad ingredients and add seasonings.
22. Mix dressings with salad ingredients. Mix thoroughly and serve.

SICHUAN STYLE BRAISED EGGPLANT WITH PICKLED CHILIES AND GARLIC

INGREDIENTS

- 2 tablespoons Sichuan chili
- Roughly cilantro leaves
- 4 medium garlic
- 4 scallions
- Kosher salt
- 1 ½ pounds Chinese eggplants
- 3 tablespoons vegetable oil
- 4 teaspoons minced fresh ginger
- 2 red Thai bird chilies
- 1 tablespoon Chinkiang vinegar
- 1 ¼ teaspoons cornstarch
- 3 tablespoons white vinegar
- 1 tablespoon sugar
- 2 teaspoons soy sauce
- 2 tablespoons Shaoxing wine

INSTRUCTIONS

1. In a medium mixing bowl, combine ½ cup kosher salt and 2 quarts of water.
2. Toss in the eggplant slices.
3. In the meantime, in a medium bowl, heat white vinegar until it begins to boil.
4. In a small cup, place cut chilies and pour boiling vinegar over them.
5. After that, combine the wine, sugar, sesame oil, and Chinkiang vinegar in a mixing bowl.
6. Cautiously drain the eggplant and allow it to dry with paper towels.
7. In a skillet, heat the oil over high heat until it begins to smoke.
8. Cook with the eggplant. Toss to the sides of the wok.
9. Add the ginger, garlic, and green onions to the wok and return it to high heat.
10. Cook the broad bean paste. Add the chili sauce.
11. Mix thoroughly in a serving bowl, garnish with chopped fresh, dried basil.

COOK TIME: *30 mins*
SERVING: *4*

HOT AND NUMBING XIÁN OVEN FRIED CHICKEN WINGS

INGREDIENTS

- ½ cup cilantro leaves
- 4 scallions
- 1 tablespoon brown sugar
- 2 teaspoons vegetable oil
- 4 pounds chicken wings
- 1 tablespoon red pepper flakes
- 1 tablespoon Sichuan peppercorns
- 1 tablespoon baking powder
- 1 tablespoon whole cumin seed
- 1 teaspoon whole fennel seed
- 1 ½ tablespoon kosher salt

COOK TIME: 25 mins
SERVING: 4

INSTRUCTIONS

1. Use paper towels, gently dry the chicken wings.
2. Toss one teaspoon rice flour and one teaspoon salt in a wide mixing bowl until completely and uniformly coated.
3. Place the baking sheet with the wings in the refrigerator for at least 8 hours, covered.
4. Preheat the oven to 450 degrees Fahrenheit.
5. Cook for 20 minutes after adding the chicken wings.
6. In a cup, combine ground spices and flavorings.
7. Move the wings to a big mixing bowl and toss with oil until they are finished.
8. Half of the spice powder and all of the coriander and green onions should be added.
9. Taste one wing and season with more spice powder as required. Serve right away.

CHINESE BEAN CURD ROLLS STUFFED WITH PORK, GINGER AND MUSHROOMS

INGREDIENTS

- **For the Rolls**
- 3 ½ ounces enoki mushrooms
- 1 small carrot
- 3 teaspoons vegetable oil
- 6 sheets bean-curd skin
- 1-ounce shiitake mushroom
- 1 teaspoon sugar
- 1 teaspoon cornstarch
- 1 teaspoon soy sauce
- **For the Pork Filling**
- ½ teaspoon kosher salt
- ½ teaspoon sugar
- 1 teaspoon Shaoxing wine
- ½ teaspoon fresh ginger
- ½ pound ground pork
- 1 teaspoon minced garlic

INSTRUCTIONS

1. Combine all of the components in a big mixing bowl and stir well.
2. Put it in the fridge for at least 30 minutes, or up to 24 hours.
3. Combine the shiitake mushrooms, sesame oil, sugar, cornflour, and one teaspoon of oil in a mixing bowl. Refrigerate until ready to use.
4. Use two heaping tablespoons of meat filling, make a sandwich.
5. Organize the vegetable and mushroom fillings in a nice pattern.
6. Pull the bean curd skin texture to edge over the liquid.
7. Roll the bean curd covering tightly toward you and shape a neat roll.
8. Heat the remaining two teaspoons of oil in a small saucepan.
9. Make bean-curd rolls in the oven. Place on a plate and set aside to cool for five minutes.
10. Stir together the sauce ingredients and cook until it thickens.
11. Make a steamer. Toss the bean curd rolls in the sauce.
12. Serve the remaining green onion on top of the rolls.

- 1 teaspoon soy sauce
- ¼ ounce wood ear mushrooms
- 1 ½ teaspoons cornstarch
- 2 teaspoons sesame oil

For the Sauce

- 1 teaspoon sesame oil
- 2 scallions
- 2 teaspoons cornstarch
- ¼ cup water
- 1 cup chicken stock
- ½ teaspoon minced garlic
- ½ teaspoon sugar
- 1 teaspoon Shaoxing wine
- 1 teaspoon oyster sauce
- 1 teaspoon soy sauce

COOK TIME: 30 mins
SERVING: 4

CRYSTAL SKIN SHRIMP DUMPLINGS

INGREDIENTS

- **For the Dough**
- ⅛ teaspoon salt
- 2 teaspoons vegetable oil
- 6 tablespoon tapioca flour
- ¾ cup wheat starch
- ½ cup water
- **For the Shrimp Filling**
- 1 teaspoon cornstarch
- Black vinegar for serving
- ¼ teaspoon white pepper
- 1 teaspoon oil
- ¼ teaspoon salt
- ¼ teaspoon sugar
- ½ pound shrimp
- ½ teaspoon minced garlic
- ½ teaspoon Shaoxing wine
- 1 teaspoon baking soda
- ½ teaspoon minced ginger
- 1 pork fatback

COOK TIME: 60 mins
SERVING: 24

INSTRUCTIONS

1. ½ cup of water should be brought to a boil.
2. Combine wheat starch, tapioca cornstarch, and salt in a mixing dish.
3. Combine the flour mixture in a mixing bowl.
4. Combine the oil and the warm water in a mixing bowl.
5. Mix until a loose dough forms with a spatula.
6. Wrap shrimp in cold water and add white vinegar to a medium mixing bowl.
7. Put it in the fridge for 30 minutes before serving.
8. Place the shrimp in a bowl, cut into four to five sections.
9. Salt, sugar, grounded white pepper, oil, and corn flour are combined with minced fatback, diced ginger, garlic powder, Shaoxing wine, seasoning, sugar, ground black pepper, oil, and rice flour.
10. Combine all of the ingredients in a large mixing bowl and set them aside in the fridge.
11. Cut the dough into twelve parts, each weighing around ¼ ounce.

27. Wrap the bags in plastic wrap

12. Wrap the bags in plastic wrap before you are ready to fill them.
13. To assemble the wrappers, position three to four pieces of seafood in each wrapper's center, along with the fatback.
14. Sear the edge with a small fork.
15. Set up a wok to prepare the dumplings.
16. Every batch of dumplings should be steamed for 7 minutes over medium temperature.
17. Allow five minutes for the dumplings to rest before serving with black vinegar.

GROUND PORK AND CORN CONGEE

INGREDIENTS

- ½ cup short grain rice
- About 1 cup corn
- 2 scallions, chopped
- 6 cups water
- ½ pound ground pork
- 1 ½ teaspoons cornstarch
- 2 teaspoons vegetable oil
- ½ teaspoon minced fresh ginger
- ¼ teaspoon sugar
- ½ teaspoon soy sauce
- ½ teaspoon minced garlic
- Kosher salt
- 1 teaspoon Shaoxing wine

COOK TIME: *30 mins*
SERVING: *4*

INSTRUCTIONS

1. Add meat, spice, cloves, and Shaoxing wine, ¼ teaspoon of salt, sugar, sesame oil, cornstarch, and oil in a mixing bowl.
2. Combine all of the ingredients in a large mixing bowl and set them aside in the fridge.
3. Fill a big pot halfway with water and add the cleaned rice. Make sure the rice is not stuck to the bottom by stirring it.
4. Thirty minutes after the first swirl, cover the pot and then stir the rice once more.
5. Cover the pot once more and cook for another thirty minutes.
6. When the congee is finished, it should have a smooth, silky texture.
7. Boil for ten minutes after adding the ground pork to the congee and bringing it down.
8. Turn the heat down, add the corn, and spice the congee with salt and pepper to taste. Mix thoroughly with green onion sliced on top.

VEGETABLE AND NOODLE OMELET

INGREDIENTS

- 2 teaspoons sesame oil
- 1 tablespoon soy sauce
- 800g packet stir-fry vegetable
- 1 tablespoon oyster sauce
- 2 garlic cloves
- 2cm piece fresh ginger
- 100g rice vermicelli noodles
- 2 green onions
- 1 ½ tablespoon vegetable oil
- 8 eggs

COOK TIME: 10 mins
SERVING: 4

INSTRUCTIONS

1. In a heatproof pan, position the noodles.
2. Fill the pot halfway with boiling water.
3. Wait for 3 - 4 minutes, or until the vegetables are soft.
4. Drain the water. In a mixing bowl, whisk together the eggs and onions.
5. In a slow cooker, heat two teaspoons peanut oil over medium temperature.
6. To coat, swirl it around. Garlic and ginger should be added now.
7. Combine the vegetable mixture, oyster sauce, and soy sauce in a mixing bowl.
8. In a 20cm nonstick roasting tray, heat one teaspoon of the residual vegetable oil over medium-high heat.
9. One-quarter of the beaten egg should be added.
10. Heat for 30 seconds, or until the sauce is barely set.
11. One-quarter of the vegetable mixture should be placed on one-half of the omelets.
12. Cook for 1 minute, or until the egg is fully set.
13. To make four omelets, repeat with the remaining oil, beaten eggs, and vegetable combination.
14.

NO COOK CHICKEN BANH MI

INGREDIENTS

- 1 tablespoon sriracha or chili sauce
- 8 long coriander sprigs
- ½ Coles hot roast chicken
- 200g packet Coles beetroot slaw
- ½ cup whole-egg mayonnaise
- 4 Coles Vietnamese rolls

COOK TIME: 15 mins
SERVING: 4

INSTRUCTIONS

1. After cutting all the way across, break each bread wrap in half.
2. Mayonnaise should be spread on the cut ends.
3. Fill with beetroot pesto and meat.
4. If needed, sprinkle with chili sauce.
5. Serve with sprigs of cilantro.

SCRAMBLED EGG CURRY WITH TOMATO SALSA

INGREDIENTS

- Mango chutney
- Chapatti bread
- 8 eggs
- Low-fat Greek yogurt
- 200g grape tomatoes
- ½ teaspoon garam masala
- ¼ teaspoon turmeric
- 12 fresh curry leaves
- 1 small brown onion
- 1 ½ tablespoon grapeseed oil
- ½ cup coriander leaves
- ¾ teaspoon cumin seeds
- ½ teaspoon mustard seeds
- 1 tablespoon lemon juice
- 3 garlic cloves

COOK TIME: 30 mins
SERVING: 4

INSTRUCTIONS

1. In a heatproof cup, position the tomato.
2. In a wide nonstick roasting tray, heat two teaspoons of the oils over moderate flame. One garlic clove and bay leaves should be added at this stage.
3. Heat for 1 minute, or until the aromas are released.
4. Pour over the tomato as soon as possible.
5. In the same pan, heat the remaining oil over moderate flame.
6. For two minutes, or until fragrant, stir in cumin seeds.
7. Add the onion and cook for three minutes, or until tender.
8. Stir in the additional garlic and chili for 1 minute, or until fragrant.
9. For two minutes, or until aromatic, stir in the spice and fenugreek.
10. Pour the egg into the pan—Cook for thirty seconds without stirring.
11. Serve with salsa verde, yogurt, sorbet, and chapatti on the side.

ASIAN PRAWN OMELET

INGREDIENTS

- 2 long red chilies
- 1 cup coriander leaves
- 1 large carrot
- 2 spring onions
- 8 eggs
- 24 green king prawns
- 1 red onion
- 3 teaspoons fish sauce
- 80ml peanut oil
- 80g butter
- **Dressing**
- 1 tablespoon caster sugar
- 1 long red chili, seeded
- 2 limes
- 1 tablespoon fish sauce
- 2 cloves garlic

COOK TIME: 30 mins
SERVING: 2

INSTRUCTIONS

1. To make the dressing, whisk together all of the components in a small mixing bowl until well mixed.
2. To make omelets, whisk together eggs, shrimp paste, and two tablespoons of cold water in a mixing bowl.
3. In a deep fryer, heat one tablespoon oil and 20g fat over medium–high heat. Cook, sometimes flipping, with six shrimp and a quarter of the onions.
4. One-quarter of the egg mix should be added. Add salt and pepper to taste.
5. To keep the omelets soft, transfer them to a plate and coat them loosely with tape.
6. Toss the vegetables, green onions, bell peppers, and coriander with half of the dressing in a large mixing bowl.
7. Serve the omelets on plates with the salad combination on top.
8. To eat, drizzle with the leftover dressing.

BANH XEO (CRISPY PANCAKES)

INGREDIENTS

- Butter lettuce leaves
- Fresh mint leaves
- 220g rice flour
- 12 cooked prawns
- 130g bean sprouts
- 1 brown onion
- 300g Pork Porterhouse Steak
- 2 tablespoons cornflour
- Pinch of white pepper
- 2 tablespoons peanut oil
- 1 can coconut milk
- 1 teaspoon sugar
- ½ teaspoon salt
- 1 teaspoon ground turmeric
- 310ml iced water

Nuoc Cham
- 1 long chili
- 1 garlic clove
- 1 ½ tablespoons water
- 1 tablespoon caster sugar
- 60ml fresh lime juice
- 60ml fish sauce

INSTRUCTIONS

1. In a small cup, mix the fish sauce, lemon juice, water, butter, chili, and garlic. Mix until the sugar is fully dissolved.
2. In a medium mixing bowl, add flour mixture, coconut milk, water, turmeric, sugar, and salt.
3. Cover and chill for 1 hour or overnight to allow flavors to meld.
4. Preheat a nonstick deep fryer with a 20cm diameter over high heat.
5. Heat 1 tablespoon of oil until it just starts to smoke.
6. Three minutes, or until translucent, stir-fry the onion and meat.
7. One-quarter of the remaining oil should be lightly brushed over the pan. One-quarter of the flour mix should be added now.
8. Three minutes in the oven, half the pancake should be filled with one-quarter of the pork combination and one-quarter of the prawns.
9. To seal the envelope, fold it over. Cover with foil and move to a tray.
10. Serve with lettuce on the side.

COOK TIME: 30 mins
SERVING: 8

PEKING CHICKEN SALAD WITH SNOW PEA SALAD

INGREDIENTS

- 400g packet French-style crepes
- 8 garlic chives
- 3 cups cooked chicken
- 2/3 cup hoisin sauce
- 150g snow peas
- 50g snow pea sprouts
- 2 Lebanese cucumbers
- 4 green onions

COOK TIME: 20 mins
SERVING: 4

INSTRUCTIONS

1. Snow peas should be finely shredded, and onions should be thinly sliced.
2. Place in a mixing bowl. Toss in the cucumber and sprouts.
3. Toss all together. Separate the chicken and the hoisin sauce into two containers.
4. Crepes should be heated according to the instructions on the package.
5. On a tray, place one crepe. One-eighth of the snow pea combination, chicken, and hoisin sauce should be on top.
6. Using a chive, secure the chive.
7. Replace the crepes, snow pea combination, and hoisin sauce with the leftover crepes, snow pea combination, and hoisin sauce. Serve the food.

CHICKEN GINGER CONGEE

INGREDIENTS

- 2 teaspoons fried garlic
- Soy sauce to serve
- ½ teaspoon sesame oil
- 1 tablespoon fried shallots
- Salt and ground white pepper
- 2 tablespoons green onion
- 1-liter chicken liquid stock
- 200g chicken tenderloin
- 1 teaspoon Chinese rice wine
- 500ml water
- ½ cup long grain rice
- 4 slices of young ginger

INSTRUCTIONS

1. In a wide heavy-based frying pan, carry the chicken broth, water, and spice to a boil over medium temperature.
2. Reduce heat to medium-low and add the garlic.
3. Cook, wrapped, for 1 hour, just until the rice has browned and most of the water has been drained, stirring regularly to prevent the rice from sticking.
4. Simmer for 4-5 minutes, just until the meat is just cooked, after adding the meat to the congee.
5. Dress the congee with salt and pepper after adding the rice wine.
6. Spray the spring onions on top of the congee, sprinkled with sesame oil, and finish with the caramelized onion and garlic.
7. Serve with a side of soy sauce.

COOK TIME: 70 mins
SERVING: 4

KIMCHI FRIED RICE WITH BACON AND EGGS

INGREDIENTS

- 30g unsalted butter
- Thinly sliced garlic chives
- 2 teaspoon sesame oil
- 2 teaspoon soy sauce
- 1 tablespoon rice bran oil
- 4 cups white rice
- 4 eggs
- 1 small onion
- 1 cup kimchi
- 2 tablespoon kimchi juice
- 4 bacon rashers
- 2 garlic cloves
- 1 cup fresh peas
- 1 tablespoon ginger

INSTRUCTIONS

1. In a skillet, heat the rice bran oil over moderate flame.
2. For 3-4 minutes, cook, medium heat, or till onions are soft and bacon is crispy.
3. Cook for thirty minutes, after adding the ginger and garlic.
4. Cook by constantly stirring, for two minutes, until peas, sushi, and riceare well cooked. Remove from the heat.
5. In a frying pan, heat the oil over medium-high heat. 2 shells, carefully broken into oil and fried until finished. Remove using a slotted spoon.
6. Return the wok to a moderate heat area.
7. Stir in the soy sauce, sesame oil, butter, and preserved kimchi juices to warm it up.
8. To serve, divide the rice between bowls and top with a poached egg and garlic thyme.

COOK TIME: 15 mins
SERVING: 4

CHINESE FRIED EGGS WITH STICKY GINGER RICE

INGREDIENTS

- 1 long fresh red chili
- Steamed Asian greens
- 2 ½ tablespoons oyster sauce
- 2 green shallots
- 1 tablespoon grapeseed oil
- Grapeseed oil
- 4 eggs
- 1 ½ tablespoons fresh ginger
- 500ml water
- 1 chicken stock cube
- 250g jasmine rice
- 1 garlic clove

COOK TIME: 20 mins
SERVING: 4

INSTRUCTIONS

1. In a frying pan, heat the oil over moderate flame.
2. Combine the ginger and garlic in a bowl.
3. Add the rice and mix well.
4. Fill the pot halfway with water and add the stock cube.
5. Get the water to a boil. Lessen to low heat and cook for 12 minutes, uncovered, or until rice is soft.
6. Cover and set aside for five minutes. Toss the rice with a fork to fluff it up.
7. In the meantime, fill a big, deep frying pan with enough extra grapeseed oil to come 1.5cm up the rim.
8. Heat over a medium-high heat area. Toss two eggs into the hot oil.
9. Cook for two minutes, or until golden brown, puffy, and the white is just set.
10. Continue with the leftover eggs.
11. Serve the rice with an egg on top of each plate.
12. Drizzle oyster sauce over the top and top with shallots and chili. Serve with boiled greens on the side.

SWEET AND SOUR EGGS

INGREDIENTS

- 2 dried bay leaves
- White pepper, to season
- 1 tablespoon brown sugar
- One teaspoon tamarind puree
- 125ml peanut oil
- 1 tablespoon sambal oelek
- 125ml water
- 6 eggs
- 3 garlic cloves
- 1 brown onion

COOK TIME: 15 mins
SERVING: 6

INSTRUCTIONS

1. In a skillet, heat the canola oil over moderate flame.
2. Cook for two minutes, or until golden brown, adding one egg at a time.
3. Cook for another thirty seconds on the other hand.
4. Repeat with the remaining egg and move to a dish.
5. In the same wok, add the ginger and garlic.
6. Stir-fry for three minutes or until the onion turns a golden brown shade.
7. Stir in the sambal oelek until all is well combined.
8. Combine the water, sugar, tamarind puree, and star anise in a large mixing bowl. Get the water to a boil.
9. Reduce the heat to a medium-low setting.
10. Cook for three minutes, or until the sauce thickness increases, before adding the eggs.
11. Add salt and white pepper to taste. Place on a plate to cool.

Chapter 4: Chinese Snack Recipes

SWEET AND SPICY SNACKS

INGREDIENTS

- ½ teaspoon onion powder
- 2 teaspoons salt
- 2-4 tablespoons hot sauce
- ½ teaspoon garlic powder
- 5 cups corn
- ¼ cup Worcestershire sauce
- ⅓ cup honey or maple syrup
- 1 cup unsalted cashews
- ½ cup butter
- 2 cups mini pretzels
- 1 cup peanuts
- 1 cup almonds
- 2 cups bagel chips

INSTRUCTIONS

1. Preheat the oven to 250 degrees Fahrenheit.
2. On a big sheet plate, mix the Chex noodles, pretzels, croissant chips, peanuts, oats, and cashew nuts.
3. Add butter, Balsamic vinegar, sugar or golden syrup, sour cream, garlic powder, smoked paprika, and salt in a small saucepan placed over medium heat.
4. Heat until the butter is fully melted and the mixture is completely smooth.
5. Rub over the Chex mixture and stir to ensure that it is evenly covered.
6. Cook for about 1 to 2 hours, mixing every ten minutes or so, till the snack mix is crispy and fluffy.
7. Allow cooling fully before serving. For several months, store in an airtight bag.

COOK TIME: 90 mins
SERVING: 16

ONE-BOWL CARAMEL SNACK CAKE

INGREDIENTS

- 1 teaspoon vanilla extract
- Flaky sea salt
- ¾ teaspoon salt
- ¼ cup confectioners' sugar
- 1 ½ teaspoons baking powder
- ¼ teaspoon baking soda
- Cooking oil spray
- 1 cup all-purpose flour
- ¾ cup cake flour
- 2 large egg yolks
- 1 cup heavy cream
- ¾ cup unsalted butter
- 1 tablespoon vanilla extract
- 1 large egg
- 1/3 cup heavy cream
- 1 teaspoon flaky sea salt
- 1 cup dark brown sugar

COOK TIME: 45 mins
SERVING: 6

INSTRUCTIONS

1. Preheat the oven to 350 degrees Fahrenheit.
2. Use cooking oil mist, spray an 8-inch square plate.
3. Microwave on high for 1 minute, or until butter is melted.
4. Set aside half a cup of the mixture in a big mixing bowl.
5. To the leftover ¼ cup melted butter, add milk and then cinnamon.
6. Mix the sugar, cinnamon, and preserved melted butter in a blending bowl until smooth.
7. Pour in the milk and the caramel sauce.
8. Place the flour mixture into the wet using the sheet.
9. Preheat the oven to 350°F and bake the cake for 20 minutes on the middle rack.
10. Caramel toppings are added, then slices are split and served.

CHINESE STYLE BRAISED BOK CHOY

INGREDIENTS

- Steamed bok choy
- Steamed basmati rice
- 3 tablespoon dark soy sauce
- 500ml beef stock
- 3-4 tablespoon olive oil
- 2 teaspoon light sugar
- 3 tablespoon Chinese cooking wine
- 6 garlic cloves
- 1 teaspoon Chinese five-spice powder
- 2-star anise
- Thumb-size root ginger
- 1 ½kg braising beef
- 2 tablespoon plain flour
- 1 red chili
- 1 bunch spring onions

INSTRUCTIONS

1. In a big, deep casserole, heat two tablespoons of the oil.
2. Cook the garlic, onions, peppers, and chili in a skillet.
3. Toss the meat in flour, then apply one tablespoon of further oil to the pan and brown in batches.
4. Toss in the five-spice and star anise, then the gingery mixture.
5. Preheat the oven to 150 degrees Celsius.
6. Put in the soy and storage, bring to a boil, then cover loosely and cook in the oven.
7. Add more soy sauce to taste.
8. Place the cooked Bok choy in the bowl, then immediately carry to the table with the brown rice and eat.

COOK TIME: 120 mins
SERVING: 4

CHINESE MEAT FILLED BUNS

INGREDIENTS

- 2 ½ tablespoons water
- One recipe Chinese steamed buns
- 1 tablespoon white sugar
- Ground black pepper to taste
- 8 ounces chopped pork
- 1 tablespoon rice wine
- 1 tablespoon vegetable oil
- 1 (4 ounces) can of shrimp
- 1 tablespoon fresh ginger root
- 1 tablespoon light soy sauce
- 2 green onions
- 1 teaspoon salt

COOK TIME: 160 mins
SERVING: 4

INSTRUCTIONS

1. In a skillet, cook minced pork over medium-high heat.
2. Set aside to cool after draining and seasoning with salt.
3. Green onions, pepper, sesame oil, white wine, oil, salt, and pepper should be combined.
4. Mix in the minced beef. Add the water and completely mix it in.
5. Preheat the oven to 350°F and prepare the dough for Chinese steamed buns.
6. Form dough balls and tie them around the filling.
7. In a skillet, bring the water to a boil and then reduce the heat to low.
8. Place as many buns on parchment paper as possible.
9. Then use a lid, cover the wok.
10. Heat buns for 20 to 30 minutes over hot water.
11. Steam the buns in groups until they are all finished.

CHINESE CHICKEN AND MUSHROOMS

INGREDIENTS

- **For the Stir Fry**
- 2 green onions
- 1 tablespoon oil
- 2½ cups sliced mushrooms
- 1 clove garlic
- 1 ½ tablespoon bicarb of soda
- 1 lb. chicken breasts
- **For the Sauce**
- ½ teaspoon pepper
- 1 teaspoon sugar
- 1 teaspoon oyster sauce
- 2 teaspoon sesame oil
- 2 tablespoon Chinese cooking wine
- 2 tablespoon soy sauce
- 3 tablespoon cornstarch
- ¾ cup cold chicken stock

COOK TIME: 31 mins
SERVING: 4

INSTRUCTIONS

1. Around the grain, cut the meat into small slices.
2. Spray the baking soda over the meat in a mixing bowl and slowly pour to cover.
3. Wash the meat many times to remove the baking soda.
4. In a big glass container, combine all of the sauce components.
5. Put the oil in a heavy-bottomed frying pan over medium temperature.
6. Stir in the spring onions with the bell peppers in the oil.
7. Cook for 2 minutes after adding the chicken to the bowl.
8. Add the remaining mushrooms to the mix.
9. Add the garlic slices.
10. Allow the sauce a final swirl before pouring it into the pan.
11. Serve right away.

CHINESE PORK BELLY BUNS

INGREDIENTS

- Steamed Buns
- 3 tablespoon unsalted butter
- 1 tablespoon olive oil
- 2 teaspoon instant dried yeast
- 3 tablespoon whole milk
- 3 ¾ cups flour
- ½ teaspoon salt
- ¾ cup warm water
- 2 tablespoon caster sugar
- Slow-Cooked Pork Belly
- 1 tablespoon rice wine
- 1 tablespoon caster sugar
- 1 tablespoon minced ginger
- 3 cloves garlic
- 4 ¼ cups chicken stock
- 2.2 lb. rindless pork belly
- Pork Belly Glaze
- 3 tablespoon dark soy sauce
- 1 teaspoon lemongrass paste
- 2 tablespoon honey

INSTRUCTIONS

1. Begin by preparing the bao buns.
2. In a mixing bowl, combine the flour, salt, sugar, and yeast.
3. In a jug, combine the milk, hot water, and butter and whisk until the butter has melted.
4. In an oiled pan, position the dough.
5. Begin preparing the pork belly in the meantime.
6. In a pan, combine all of the ingredients for the slow-cooked pork belly.
7. Re-knead the dough and divide it into ten balls.
8. Position the buns on the baking trays in the oven.
9. Place a large wok pan over high heat and bring to a boil.
10. Slice the pork into small bite-size pieces.
11. In a deep fryer, heat one tablespoon of the oil.
12. Add the oil and insert the pork, along with the salt and black pepper, to fry at medium temperature until the pork begins to turn golden.
13. Cover the buns and fill them with a sticky pork belly once they have finished cooking. Sesame seeds should be sprinkled on top.

- 2 tablespoon brown sugar
- 2 tablespoon vegetable oil
- 1 tablespoon minced ginger
- 1 red chili
- 1 pinch of salt and pepper

COOK TIME: 150 mins
SERVING: 4

SKINNY BEEF AND BROCCOLI NOODLES

INGREDIENTS

- 400g pack beef stir-fry strips
- Sliced spring onion
- 1 head broccoli
- 1 tablespoon sesame oil
- 3 blocks egg noodles
- **For the Sauce**
- 1 thumb-sized knob ginger
- 1 tablespoon white wine vinegar
- 1 tablespoon tomato ketchup
- 2 garlic cloves
- 2 tablespoon oyster sauce
- 3 tablespoon low-salt soy sauce

INSTRUCTIONS

1. Begin by preparing the sauce.
2. In a small mixing bowl, combine all of the components.
3. Follow the package directions for boiling the noodles.
4. Add broccoli a moment before they are finished.
5. In the meantime, heat the oil in a skillet until very warm, then stir-fry the meat until well golden brown, around 2-3 minutes.
6. Pour in the sauce, give it a good stir, and leave it to simmer for a few minutes before turning off the gas.
7. Drain the noodles, toss them with the beef, and serve immediately, garnished with green onions.

COOK TIME: *30 mins*
SERVING: *4*

ASIAN STEAK ROLL-UPS

INGREDIENTS

- Kosher salt and black pepper to taste
- Sesame seeds for garnish
- 2 tablespoons olive oil
- Asian glaze
- 4 pounds steak top round
- 1 pound asparagus
- 1 red onion
- 2 large color bell peppers

COOK TIME: 35 mins
SERVING: 8

INSTRUCTIONS

1. Preheat oven to 400 degrees Fahrenheit.
2. On a work surface, lay down a few meat strips.
3. Fill each roll with a few slices of onions, peppers, and asparagus.
4. Dress the meat and veggies with salt and pepper to taste.
5. In a medium saucepan, heat the oil over medium-high heat.
6. Caramelize the steak wraps on all surfaces until they are browned.
7. Preheat the oven to 350°F and bake the steak rolls for fifteen minutes.
8. Cover with an Asian glaze to keep hot.
9. Remove the meat rolls from the stove after fifteen minutes of cooking.
10. Return the steak rolls to the oven for a final ten minutes.
11. Allow five minutes for the rolls to rest.
12. Serve with sesame seeds on top and additional sauce on the side, if needed.

SKINNY PANDA EXPRESS COPYSCAT CHOWMEIN

INGREDIENTS

- 2 celery stalks
- ½ head cabbage
- 1 tablespoon olive oil
- 1 large onion
- 1 lb. rice noodles
- 2 cloves garlic, minced
- 1 teaspoon ginger
- ½ cup soy sauce

COOK TIME: 30 mins
SERVING: 4

INSTRUCTIONS

1. Process noodles once al dente in a wide pot of boiling water as per package instructions.
2. Return to the pot after draining.
3. Combine the soy sauce, ginger, and seasoning in a small cup.
4. Heat the oil in a large frying pan.
5. Cook, medium heat, until the onion, celery, and cabbage are tender, about five to six minutes.
6. In a skillet, combine the noodles and soy sauce and mix to combine.

BEEF AND BROCCOLI STIR-FRY

INGREDIENTS

- 2 tablespoons brown sugar
- 1 teaspoon ground ginger
- 1 small onion
- 1/3 cup soy sauce
- 2 tablespoons vegetable oil
- ½ cup water
- 2 tablespoons water
- 3 tablespoons cornstarch
- 4 cups broccoli florets

COOK TIME: 25 mins

SERVING: 4

INSTRUCTIONS

1. Merge two tablespoons cornflour, two tablespoons liquid, and garlic salt in a mixing bowl and whisk until smooth.
2. Toss in the meat.
3. Stir-fry meat in 1 tablespoon oil in a pan cooker or skillet over a moderate flame until optimal doneness is reached; cut and stay warm.
4. In the cooking liquid, stir-fry the onion for 4-5 minutes or until softened.
5. Cook for another three minutes, or until the broccoli is soft but still crisp.
6. Replace the beef in the pan.
7. To make the sauce, whisk together the soy sauce, black pepper, spice, and the remaining one tablespoon cornstarch with ½ cup water until smooth; pour into the jar.
8. Serve with toasted pine nuts on top of rice.

KUNG PAO SHRIMP

INGREDIENTS

- **Stir Fry**
- 3 green onions
- ¼ cup dry roasted peanuts
- 1 tablespoon ginger
- ½ teaspoon red pepper flakes
- 2 tablespoons vegetable oil
- 1 green bell pepper
- 1 tablespoon garlic
- 1 red pepper
- 1 small onion
- **Marinade**
- 1 tbsp soy sauce
- 2 teaspoons cornstarch
- ¾ pound shrimp
- **Sauce**
- 1 teaspoon sesame oil
- 1 teaspoon cornstarch
- 1 tablespoon dry sherry
- 1 teaspoon brown sugar
- ⅓ cup chicken stock
- 2 tablespoons hoisin sauce
- ¼ cup soy sauce

COOK TIME: 40 mins
SERVING: 2

INSTRUCTIONS

1. In a small cup, combine the seafood, soy sauce, and cornflour.
2. Set aside the components for the sauce.
3. In a pan, heat the vegetable oil over a moderate flame.
4. Stir-fry the seafood for 2-3 minutes, or until it turns yellow.
5. If necessary, add additional oil to the pan before adding the onions.
6. Cook for around 2-3 minutes, or until they melt.
7. Add the garlic, ginger, and chili flakes, as well as the red and green bell peppers.
8. Cook for five minutes or until the veggies soften slightly.
9. Cook, constantly stirring, until the sauce thickens.
10. Serve over rice with spring onions and nuts.

BAKED HONEY GARLIC SKILLET CHICKEN

INGREDIENTS

- Sesame seeds, for garnish
- Scallions, for garnish
- 1 tablespoon cornstarch
- 1 lb. chicken breasts
- ¼ cup soy sauce
- 1 teaspoon sriracha
- 2 tablespoon sesame oil
- 2 cloves garlic, minced
- Juice of 1 lime
- 3 tablespoon honey

COOK TIME: 60 mins
SERVING: 4

INSTRUCTIONS

1. Preheat the oven to 350 degrees Fahrenheit.
2. Spoon combined sesame oil, sugar, garlic, lemon juice, Sriracha, one tablespoon soy sauce, and cornstarch in a medium mixing cup.
3. Season the chicken with salt and black pepper before serving.
4. Heat oil in an oven-safe saucepan over medium heat.
5. Braise the chicken for four minutes until crispy, then turn and cook for another four minutes.
6. Pour the glaze over the top and bake in the oven.
7. Bake for 25 minutes, or until meat is cooked through.
8. Broil for two minutes after sprinkling glaze over chicken.
9. Serve with spring onions and sesame seeds as garnish.

GINGER PORK POT STICKERS

INGREDIENTS

- **For Dumplings**
- 60 dumpling wrappers
- Vegetable oil
- 1 large egg, lightly beaten
- Flour, for surface
- 2 teaspoon ginger
- 2 teaspoon fish sauce
- 1 lb. ground pork
- 2 tablespoon low-sodium soy sauce
- 2 teaspoon sesame oil
- ¼ cup chicken broth
- 2 cloves garlic
- 2 green onions
- **For Dipping Sauce**
- 3 tablespoon rice wine vinegar
- ¼ cup soy sauce

COOK TIME: 95 mins
SERVING: 5 dozen

INSTRUCTIONS

1. Mix the pork, stock, white sections of spring onions, ginger, sesame oil, soy sauce, spice, fish sauce if used, and egg in a big mixing bowl.
2. In a large frying pan, heat one tablespoon olive oil over moderate flame.
3. Dumplings should be arranged on an even surface.
4. Fry for 1–2 minutes, or until golden brown on the bottom.
5. Reduce heat to medium-low and protect with a tight-fitting lid after adding 1/3 cup water to the skillet.
6. Cook for another three minutes, or until there is no more water.
7. In a medium mixing cup, whisk together soy sauce, rice wine vinegar, and the reserved green bits of spring onions.
8. Potstickers should be served with a dipping sauce.

SHRIMP WONTONS

INGREDIENTS

- Cooking spray
- 2-4 tablespoon sweet chili sauce
- 1 tablespoon fresh chives
- 14 won-ton wrappers
- Eight large shrimp
- ½ teaspoon red pepper flakes
- ¼ teaspoon salt
- 1 clove garlic
- 2 tablespoon feta cheese
- ½ teaspoon garlic powder
- Three tablespoon cream cheese
- 1 teaspoon butter

COOK TIME: 30 mins
SERVING: 14

INSTRUCTIONS

1. Preheat the oven to 400 degrees Fahrenheit.
2. It is entirely up to you if you sauté the seafood in 1 teaspoon of olive oil or butter. Cook with the garlic.
3. Shrimp should be minced into very small bits.
4. Combine the cheeses, chives, red pepper, garlic salt, and spice in a small mixing bowl.
5. Fill each wonton with a heaping teaspoon of the seafood combination.
6. Preheat oven to 400°F and bake for 5-7 minutes until it is lightly browned.
7. Serve hot with a side of sweet chili sauce for dipping!

MOO GOO GAI PAN

INGREDIENTS

- 1 tablespoon rice wine
- ¼ cup chicken broth
- 1 tablespoon soy sauce
- 1 tablespoon cornstarch
- 1 tablespoon white sugar
- 1 tablespoon oyster sauce
- 2 cloves garlic
- 1 pound chicken breast
- 1 tablespoon vegetable oil
- 15 ounce can straw mushrooms
- 1 tablespoon vegetable oil
- 1 cup fresh mushrooms
- 8-ounce bamboo shoots
- 8-ounce water
- 2 cups broccoli florets

INSTRUCTIONS

1. In a griddle or broad skillet, heat one tablespoon olive oil over medium temperature until it starts to smoke.
2. Fresh mushrooms, lettuce, bamboo shoots, artichoke hearts, and straw shiitake should all be added at this stage.
3. Continue cooking for five minutes, or until all the veggies are hot and the lettuce is soft.
4. In the skillet, heat the remaining tablespoon of vegetables until it starts to smoke.
5. Heat for several seconds, constantly stirring, before the garlic turns lightly golden.
6. Toss in the chicken.
7. In a small cup, combine the cornstarch, sugar, sesame oil, oyster sauce, white wine, and chicken broth.
8. Cook for 30 seconds, or until the sauce has thickened.
9. Toss the veggies back into the wok with the sauce.

COOK TIME: 40 mins
SERVING: 3

Chapter 6: Chinese Dinner Recipes

CHINESE CHICKEN SKEWERS

INGREDIENTS

- Marinade
- 2 cloves garlic
- 1 ½ teaspoon fresh ginger
- 1 teaspoon sesame oil
- 1 teaspoon white sugar
- 3 tablespoon oyster sauce
- 1 tablespoon Chinese cooking wine
- 2 teaspoon sriracha sauce
- 1 tablespoon soy sauce
- Skewers
- 12 bamboo skewers
- 2 tablespoon vegetable oil
- 1.5 lb. chicken thighs

INSTRUCTIONS

1. In a mixing dish, blend the marinade components.
2. Set aside for at least thirty minutes, or up to midnight, to caramelize the chicken.
3. Use skewers, thread the chicken onto the skewers.
4. In a medium saucepan, heat one tablespoon of oil on a moderate flame.
5. Heat half of the skewers for three to five minutes on each side until it is soft, lightly browned, pressing them down with a spatula to ensure even cooking.
6. Continue with the available skewers.
7. Serve warm with thinly chopped scallions as a garnish.

COOK TIME: 45 mins
SERVING: 4

SESAME CHINESE CHICKEN WITH RICE

INGREDIENTS

- **Sauce**
- 2 tablespoon brown sugar
- 4 tablespoon soy sauce
- 2 tablespoon sweet chili sauce
- 3 tablespoon ketchup
- 1 tablespoon sesame oil
- 1 tablespoon Chinese rice vinegar
- 1 tablespoon honey
- 2 cloves garlic
- **Other Ingredients**
- 2 teaspoon paprika
- 3 chicken breast fillets
- ½ teaspoon pepper
- ½ teaspoon garlic salt
- 5 tablespoon vegetable oil
- 10 tablespoon plain flour
- ½ teaspoon salt
- 3 tablespoon cornflour
- 2 eggs

INSTRUCTIONS

1. In a griddle or big frying pan, add the oil until it is very warm.
2. Put the egg in one small dish and the corn starch in another small bowl while the oil is heating.
3. In a separate shallow dish, combine the rice, salt, pepper, garlic powder, and paprika.
4. Dig the chicken in cornmeal, then in egg, and then in prepared rice.
5. In a hot wok, combine all of the sauce components, stir, and cook over high heat until the sauce has reduced by about a third.
6. Return the chicken to the pan and throw it in the sauce to coat it.
7. Cover with sesame oil and green onions and serve with steamed rice.

To Serve

- 2 tablespoon sesame seeds
- Small bunch of spring onions
- Boiled rice

COOK TIME: 30 mins
SERVING: 4

HONEY CHICKEN

INGREDIENTS

- 2 tablespoons rice wine vinegar
- 1 tablespoon soy sauce
- 1/3 cup honey
- ¼ cup water
- 6 chicken thighs
- 2 teaspoons garlic powder
- 6 cloves garlic
- Salt and pepper

COOK TIME: 30 mins
SERVING: 6

INSTRUCTIONS

1. Put aside chicken that has been seasoned with salt, pepper, and cayenne pepper.
2. Brine chicken thighs cutlets in a pan or skillet over medium-low heat.
3. Turn off the heat after both sides have been seared, protect the pan with a cover, and continue to cook.
4. Drain the majority of the residual water from the bowl, leaving about two tablespoons to add flavor.
5. Between the meats, add the onion and fry until aromatic.
6. Combine the honey, water, vinegar, and sesame oil in a mixing bowl.
7. Reduce the heat to moderate and simmer until the sauce has thickened and reduced slightly.
8. Serve over tomatoes, rice, pasta, or with a salad garnished with parsley.

EGG FOO YOUNG

INGREDIENTS

- 2 tablespoons white vinegar
- 2 tablespoons soy sauce
- 2 tablespoons cornstarch
- 2 tablespoons sugar
- 2 tablespoons vegetable oil
- 3 cups chicken broth
- 1 cup cooked small shrimp
- ¼ teaspoon garlic powder
- 4 eggs
- ⅓ cup green onions
- 8 ounces bean sprouts

COOK TIME: 20 mins
SERVING: 2

INSTRUCTIONS

1. In a mixing bowl, whisk together the eggs, black beans, spring onions, seafood, and sour cream until thoroughly mixed.
2. To create a patty, heat oil in a saucepan over medium heat and dump about half a cup of the beaten egg into the pan.
3. Repeat with the remaining beaten egg and cook until lightly browned, around three minutes per hand.
4. Remove the patties from the pan and set them aside.
5. In a pan over medium heat, stir together all the chicken stock, cornflour, sugar, mustard, and soy sauce until the liquid thickness increases and simmers, around five minutes.
6. Spread the sauce on top of the patties.

CHINESE BBQ PORK BUNS

INGREDIENTS

- For the Filling
- 2 tablespoons all-purpose flour
- 2 cups Chinese roast pork
- 2 teaspoons dark soy sauce
- ¾ cup chicken stock
- 2 tablespoons vegetable oil
- 2 tablespoons oyster sauce
- 1 ½ teaspoon sesame oil
- ½ cup shallots
- 2 teaspoons light soy sauce
- 2 tablespoons sugar
- For the Dough
- One tablespoon active dry yeast
- 1 ½ teaspoons salt
- ½ cup cake flour
- 3 ½ cups bread flour

INSTRUCTIONS

1. Begin with the crème Fraiche, milk, and egg, all of which should be at ambient temperature.
2. Then, add the milk, pastry flour, bread, yeast, and spice within this order.
3. To put the dough around, switch the mixer to the lowest position.
4. Form a ball out of the dough. Protect for 75-90 minutes in a hot environment.
5. Combine the rest of the ingredients with the roasted pork.
6. Transfer the filling from the skillet onto a large plate after turning off the heat.
7. Cut the dough into 16 bits that are all the same size.
8. Roll it into a 4-inch disc, significant in the middle than the corners.
9. Cover the bun with 1 part of the filling.
10. Preheat oven to 350°F and bake for 22-25 minutes until it is lightly browned.

- 2/3 cup heavy cream
- 1 large egg
- 1/3 cup sugar
- 1 cup milk
- To Finish the Buns
- 1 tablespoon sesame seeds
- 1 tablespoon granulated sugar
- Egg wash

COOK TIME: 4 hours
SERVING: 16 buns

BAKED SWEET AND SOUR CHICKEN, PINEAPPLE, CARROTS AND BELL PEPPER

INGREDIENTS

- Sweet and Sour Sauce
- ½ teaspoon red pepper flakes
- ½ teaspoon ginger powder
- 4 garlic cloves
- 1 teaspoon salt
- ½ cup pineapple juice
- 1 small onion
- 2 tablespoons soy sauce
- 1 ½ cups sugar
- ¼ cup ketchup
- 1 cup red wine vinegar
- Chicken Breading
- ¼ teaspoon ginger powder
- ¼ teaspoon onion powder
- ½ teaspoon salt
- ¼ teaspoon pepper
- 3-4 chicken breasts
- 1 1/3 cup cornstarch

INSTRUCTIONS

1. In a small saucepan, combine the components for the "Sweet and Sour Sauce," mix to combine, bring to the boil, then decrease to a gentle simmer.
2. Preheat the oven to 350 degrees Fahrenheit.
3. In a big mixing bowl, mix the eggs and set them aside.
4. In a small cup, whisk together the cornflour, garlic salt, salt, pepper, spice powder, and smoked paprika; set aside beside flour.
5. Combine the chicken and the eggs.
6. Move the meat in the bag in the freezer to uniformly coat it in cornstarch.
7. Cook for 1-2 minutes per pound of chicken.
8. Toss in the carrots, mango, and pepper with the sweetness and spice until everything is well mixed.
9. Cook, stirring regularly, for half an hour, or until sauce thickness increases.

- ½ teaspoon garlic powder
- ½ cup flour
- 3 eggs

Vegetables

- 1 red bell pepper
- 1 cup carrots sliced
- 1 green bell pepper
- 1-20 oz. can pineapple

COOK TIME: 45 mins
SERVING: 4

CHINESE CABBAGE STIR-FRY

INGREDIENTS

- 1 tablespoon soy sauce
- 1 tablespoon Chinese cooking wine
- 2 cloves garlic, minced
- 1 pound shredded cabbage
- 1 tablespoon vegetable oil

COOK TIME: 15 mins
SERVING: 4

INSTRUCTIONS

1. In a slow cooker or big skillet, steam the vegetable oil over medium-high heat.
2. Add ginger and garlic.
3. Heat for a few moments, constantly stirring, before the garlic starts to brown.
4. Wrap the skillet and cook over medium heat after stirring in the cabbage until it is fully coated in oil.
5. Continue cooking for another minute after adding the soy sauce.
6. Mix in the Chinese cooking wine and raise the heat to be large.
7. Cook and stir for another two minutes, just until the cabbage is soft.

GRILLED CHINESE CHAR SIU CHICKEN

INGREDIENTS

- Scant two teaspoons sesame oil
- 1 ¾ pounds chicken thighs
- 1 ½ tablespoons soy sauce
- 1 tablespoon ketchup
- 1 large garlic clove
- 2 tablespoons honey
- 2 tablespoons hoisin sauce
- ¼ teaspoon Chinese five-spice powder

COOK TIME: 65 mins
SERVING: 4

INSTRUCTIONS

1. Combine the garlic, five-spice mixture, butter, hoisin, sesame oil, tomato soup, and cardamom oil in a large mixing bowl.
2. Three tablespoons of the sauce should be put down for glazing the meat.
3. Add the meat to the bowl and cover it thoroughly.
4. Cover with cling film and leave to marinate to room temperature for 30 minutes.
5. Set a cast-iron kettle grill skillet over medium heat and gently oil it.
6. Cook for 7 to 9 minutes, rotating the meat many times.
7. Organize a large charcoal fire or heat it a gas grill to high and cook chicken for 8 to 10 minutes, basting every 3 minutes.
8. Before serving, move to a platter and set aside for ten minutes.

Chapter 7: Chinese Dessert Recipes

<u>ALMOND JELLY</u>

INGREDIENTS

- ¾ cup sugar
- 1 ½ teaspoons almond extract
- 1 cup water
- 2 cups milk
- 2 (.25 ounce) gelatin powder
- 1 cup water

COOK TIME: 30 mins
SERVING: 6

INSTRUCTIONS

1. In a mixing bowl, add 1 cup water, scatter the gelatin over it, and mix until the gelatin is partly absorbed.
2. Remove from the heat.
3. In a big saucepan, carry 1 cup mixture to a boil.
4. Reduce heat to moderate and add the gelatin solution gradually.
5. Pour the milk, sugars, and almond extracts into a wide, shallow container and mix until the glucose and gelatin are dissolved completely.
6. Put it in the fridge for 3 to 4 hours, or until strong.
7. To eat, cut into small pieces.

RED BEAN POPSICLES

INGREDIENTS

- 25g caster sugar
- 100g sweet red bean paste
- 125ml cream
- 2 egg yolks
- 250ml milk

COOK TIME: 35 mins
SERVING: 6

INSTRUCTIONS

1. In a small saucepan, carry the milk and butter to a low boil.
2. Remove the pan from the heat and set it aside.
3. In a mixing bowl, whisk together two egg yolks and sugars till the combination is light and moist.
4. Mix in the sweet red condensed milk with the glucose and yolk combination.
5. Load the warm wet ingredients into the beaten egg in a steady stream, constantly whisking until smooth.
6. Spoon the sauce into a large casserole dish and cook for five minutes on low heat, stirring constantly.
7. Freeze it in the refrigerator.
8. Fill an ice cream maker halfway with the chilled combination.
9. For about twenty minutes, run the ice cream machine.

FA GAO

INGREDIENTS

- ¼ cup rice flour
- 1 tablespoon baking powder
- ¼ cup neutral oil
- 1 ¼ cups all-purpose flour
- ½ cup dark brown sugar

COOK TIME: 20 mins
SERVING: 10

INSTRUCTIONS

1. Position a 10-inch wooden or steel steamer bucket in a 12-inch pan or skillet filled with around 2 inches of water.
2. In a food processor or blender, whisk together the brown sugar, oil, and ¾ cup warm water until the sugar is dissolved, around 1 minute.
3. Scroll the all-purpose flour and corn starch into the sugar syrup in three batches, stirring between each inclusion until no dry spots remain.
4. Fill the egg tart molds to the tip.
5. Under medium temperature, bring water in the pan to a gentle simmer.
6. Place the molds on a cooling rack to clear.
7. Repeat the bubbling process with the remaining five molds in the steamer basket.
8. Hot or at ambient temperature, prepare the cakes.

PINEAPPLE BUNS

INGREDIENTS

- **For the Topping Dough**
- 1 egg yolk
- ⅛ teaspoon vanilla extract
- ¼ cup vegetable shortening
- 2 tablespoons milk
- ¼ cup nonfat dry milk powder
- ¼ teaspoon baking powder
- 2/3 cup superfine sugar
- ½ teaspoon baking soda
- 1¼ cups all-purpose flour
- **For the Bread**
- 1 tablespoon active dry yeast
- 1 ½ tspsalt
- ½ cup cake flour
- 3 ½ cups bread flour
- 2/3 cup heavy cream
- 1 large egg
- 1/3 cup sugar
- 1 cup milk
- **To Finish the Buns**
- 1 egg yolk

INSTRUCTIONS

11. Begin by making the dough for the bread.
12. Combine the dough components in the bucket of an electric mixer.
13. The dough is prepared for proofing after fifteen minutes.
14. Allow the buns to rise for the next hour under a clean, wet kitchen towel.
15. In a measuring dish, add the dry powdered milk.
16. Combine the flour, white vinegar, icing sugar, and superfine sugar in a large mixing bowl.
17. To mix, stir all together.
18. Combine the shortening, butter, egg yolk, and vanilla essence in a mixing bowl.
19. Heat the oven to 350 degrees F once the buns have finished growing a second time.
20. Divide the coating dough into 12 equal portions and roll each into a ball.
21. Rub with egg white and cook for 12-13 minutes at 350 degrees.

COOK TIME: 2 hours
SERVING: 12

MUNG BEAN CAKE

INGREDIENTS

- 110g sugar
- A small pinch of salt
- 40g butter
- 50g vegetable oil
- 250g yellow mung beans
- Coloring
- 5-8 g Matcha powder

COOK TIME: 60 mins
SERVING: 1

INSTRUCTIONS

1. The yellow mung beans should be pre-soaked overnight.
2. Add enough clean water to cover the mung beans in a medium-slow cooker partially.
3. Cook according to the bean method until the beans are light and easy to break.
4. Then, using a spoon, mash them together until you have a nice and fine blend. Place it in a nonstick skillet.
5. Toss the mung bean combination with a pinch of salt, oil, and cooking oil.
6. Heat over medium-low heat, stirring constantly.
7. When the oil has been fully absorbed, add the sugar.
8. Gradually stir till they can comfortably stick together. Switch the stove off.
9. Then, using a spatula, pass the solution to a filter.
10. If you want to have more, pour the dough into shorter doughs of 30g to 40g and cover ten fillings.
11. Use a mooncake mold or some other mold to shape the mooncakes.
12. This phase should be performed when the combination is warm and not hot.

SESAME SEED BALL

INGREDIENTS

- ¼ cup sesame seeds
- 4 cups peanut oil
- ¼ cup room temperature water
- 7 ounces lotus paste
- 1 ½ cups glutinous rice flour
- ¼ cup boiling water
- 1/3 cup granulated sugar

COOK TIME: 60 mins
SERVING: 1

INSTRUCTIONS

1. To make the sesame ball flour, combine all of the ingredients in a mixing bowl.
2. In a mixing bowl, combine half a cup of glutinous rice sugar and flour.
3. Into the sugar and flour, pour ¼ cup boiling water. ¼ cup ambient temperature water and the remaining glutinous flour are added.
4. The mass of your coating should be half that of your dough ball.
5. Roll the ball in sesame oil that has been soaked until it is fully coated.
6. In a medium deep bowl, heat 4 cups almond or soybean oil to a comfortable 320°F.
7. In a small bowl, toss four sesame balls in the liquid.
8. Fry for the next five minutes, or till they turn a soft golden color, for a maximum of 17-18 minutes.
9. To remove the oil, place the completed sesame balls in a fine-mesh sieve, cooling rack, or sheet lined with towels.
10. Allow cooling for ten minutes before serving.

SACHIMA

INGREDIENTS

- **Noodle Dough**
- ⅛ teaspoon salt
- ½ teaspoon. baking soda
- 2 large eggs
- 200g all-purpose flour
- **Syrup**
- 60g maltose
- 40 water
- 130g white sugar
- **Others**
- ¼ cup cornstarch for dusting

COOK TIME: 60 mins
SERVING: 4

INSTRUCTIONS

1. Combine the all-purpose flour, brown sugar, and spice, and then stir in the egg fluid.
2. Combine all ingredients in a ball and whisk until smooth.
3. Allow the dough to rest for at least thirty minutes after covering it.
4. Heat the oil until it is extremely hot, then measure with one strip.
5. Tiny batches of strips should be fried until they are slightly orange.
6. Shake off any excess oil before placing all of the strips in a big jar.
7. Add sugar, sucrose, salt, and water in a large saucepot.
8. Warm the fluid over a moderate flame until it reaches 115 degrees Celsius.
9. By streams, pour the fluid into the flour. Mix thoroughly, attempting to cover each strip in syrup.
10. Store toppings in airtight bags and store at room temperature for up to 1 week.

Chapter 8: Chinese Soup Recipes

SIMPLE CHINESE OXTAIL SOUP

INGREDIENTS

- Salt
- Chopped cilantro
- 1 large onion
- 1 medium Chinese turnip
- 12 cups water
- 2 ½ pounds oxtails

COOK TIME: *7 hours*
SERVING: *8*

INSTRUCTIONS

1. Heat the oven to 180 degrees Celsius.
2. Clean the oxtails by rinsing them under cold water and patting them dry with a paper towel.
3. Roast for thirty minutes after arranging them on a cookie dish.
4. Add 12 cups of water to a stockpot when the oxtails are frying.
5. Bring to a boil with the vegetables and grilled oxtails.
6. Reduce the heat to a very low boil right away.
7. Cook for around 6 hours, covered, on low heat.
8. Mind to skim off the fat regularly.
9. Add the cabbages for about thirty minutes until you are ready to eat.
10. Simmer until the vegetables are tender, then season with salt and pepper to taste.
11. Serve with green onion on top.

LOTUS ROOT AND PORK SOUP

INGREDIENTS

- 12 cups cold water
- Salt 1 scallion
- 4 slices ginger
- 1 tablespoon goji berries
- 1 cup re-hydrated seaweed
- 1 pound lotus root
- 2 pounds pork ribs

COOK TIME: 7 hours
SERVING: 12

INSTRUCTIONS

1. Rinse the pork ribs or collar bones for an hour in ice water.
2. To caramelize the pork bones, bring a big pot of water to a boil.
3. Remove the pork bones from the fire, rinse, and thoroughly wash them.
4. Simply wash the salmon in a basin of water after it has been soaked until the water is clear.
5. After that, remove it and return it to the pot.
6. First, combine all of the prepared materials in a stockpot, including the pork, lotus root, seaweed, ginger, goji berries, and cold water.
7. Bring it to a boil, then reduce to low heat and keep it there.
8. Allow for at least 4 hours of simmering time.
9. Season with salt and pepper to taste, and finish with chopped green onion.

ASIAN VEGETABLE STOCK

INGREDIENTS

- ¾ cup coriander
- 6 liters cold water
- 6 celery sticks, sliced
- 10 spring onions
- 1 tablespoon sea salt
- 3 medium carrots
- 1 tablespoon vegetable oil
- 15 slices ginger
- 10 garlic cloves, crushed
- 2 medium red onions

COOK TIME: 2 hours
SERVING: 15

INSTRUCTIONS

1. In a cooking pouch, heat the oil, add the onions, garlic, cloves, salt, and cook for one minute over medium temperature.
2. Reduce heat to low and add carrots, fennel, green onions, and cardamom; cook, frequently stirring, for another three minutes or until veggies are nicely browned.
3. Take the water to a boil in the kettle.
4. Remove the stock from the heat and strain it through a muslin cloth.
5. Cool, then keep for up to three days in the fridge or three to four months in the freezer, sealed.

CHING PO LEUNG CANTONESE HERB PORK BONE SOUP

INGREDIENTS

- 3 quarts cold water
- Salt
- 2 dried honey dates
- 1 large piece of dried seafood
- 1½ pounds pork bones
- 15 grams Polygonatum datum
- 10 grams dried longan
- 4 slices fresh ginger
- 20 grams fox nut barley
- 10 grams dried goji berries
- 45 grams dried Chinese yam
- 25 grams dried lotus seeds
- 60 grams Chinese pearl barley

COOK TIME: 5 hours
SERVING: 8

INSTRUCTIONS

1. Wash the pork ribs for an hour in ice water.
2. Place the pork ribs in a large slow cooker and cover with enough ice water to fully drench them. Increase the heat to high and bring to a boil.
3. Switch off the heat after that. Also, wash the sauté pan.
4. Return the pork bones to the bath, along with the ginger, all of the dried herbs, and three quarts of ice water.
5. Bring it to a boil, then reduce to low heat and keep it there. Allow three hours for the soup to boil.
6. Skim some fat from the top of the soup before eating.
7. Season with salt and pepper, and serve immediately with soy sauce on the side for coating your pork.

CHINESE WATERCUSS SOUP WITH PORK RIBS

INGREDIENTS

- White pepper to taste
- Soy sauce to serve
- 1 to 2 bunches of watercress
- 1¼ teaspoon sea salt
- 5 slices ginger
- 8 cups water
- 1½ pounds pork rib tips or ribs

COOK TIME: 3 hours
SERVING: 4

INSTRUCTIONS

12. Blanch the bones first. Six cups of water are brought to a boil in a big pot.
13. Toss in the pulled pork. Bring the water down to a boil, then turn off the heat after two minutes.
14. In a fresh pot, combine the blanched roast pork, crushed ginger pieces, and eight glasses of water.
15. Bring the mixture to a boil, then reduce the heat to a low setting.
16. Cover and cook for 90 minutes.
17. During 90 minutes, mix in 1¼ teaspoons of pepper, lock, and boil for another thirty minutes.
18. Mix in the watercress and bring to a boil, covered.
19. Sprinkle with salt and freshly ground black pepper.
20. Serve the broth with a hot cup of porridge and a tiny dish of mild soy sauce as a side dish for the pork.

SHANGHAI STYLE RED VEGETABLE SOUP

INGREDIENTS

- 1 teaspoon black pepper
- 1 pound potatoes
- 5 bay leaves
- 2 teaspoons salt
- 2 large carrots
- ¼ cabbage
- 2 pounds oxtails
- 2 tablespoons tomato paste
- 10 cups water
- 2 tablespoons vegetable oil
- 6 cloves garlic
- 3 small tomatoes
- 2 large onions

COOK TIME: 2 hours
SERVING: 8

INSTRUCTIONS

1. Take 2 pounds of oxtails, rinse, and thoroughly dry.
2. Cook the oxtails in 2 tablespoons of oil in a dense soup saucepan over medium heat.
3. From both sides, softly brown the oxtails.
4. Break three small tomatoes into hard pieces while the onion is baking.
5. When the vegetables have weakened, add them to the bowl.
6. Turn the heat up to high and put 10 cups of water.
7. Slice the vegetables and broccoli into small pieces and combine them with five basil leaves, two teaspoons salt, and one teaspoon garlic powder in a large pot.
8. Bring to the boil, then drop to low heat and cook for 60 minutes.
9. Extract and cut the potatoes, then return them to the soup after 60 minutes of simmering. When serving, season with salt and pepper to taste.

SIMPLE WONTON SOUP

INGREDIENTS

- 6 cups chicken stock
- 1 scallion
- 2 tablespoons Shaoxing wine
- 1 package wonton wrappers
- 10 oz. baby bok choy
- 1 tablespoon soy sauce
- ½ teaspoon salt
- 8 oz. ground pork
- ⅛ teaspoon white pepper
- 2 ½ tablespoons sesame oil

COOK TIME: 2 hours
SERVING: 8

INSTRUCTIONS

1. Begin by cleaning the vegetables completely.
2. Bring a big pot of water to a boil and caramelize the vegetables for a few minutes, only before they are wilted.
3. Combine the coarsely diced vegetables, pork belly, and spices in a medium mixing dish.
4. Fill the center with a little more than a teaspoon of the coating.
5. To get a firm seal, divide the wrapper in half and bring the two sides to close.
6. To make the broth, bring your chicken stock to a boil and season with a pinch of salt and white pepper.
7. A different pot of water should be brought to a boil.
8. Continue adding the wontons to the pot a few at a time.
9. Make sure they are not overcooked.
10. Garnish with scallions after pouring the soup over the wontons. Serve it up!

CHINESE CHICKEN AND MUSHROOM SOUP

INGREDIENTS

- Salt
- 1 scallion
- 5 slices ginger
- 2 tablespoons Shaoxing wine
- 1 small organic chicken
- 1 tablespoon oil
- 20 small dried shiitake mushrooms
- 2 tablespoons dried goji berries
- 4 dried Chinese dates
- 8 cups water

COOK TIME: 90 mins
SERVING: 8

INSTRUCTIONS

11. To begin, simply wash the dried shitake mushrooms a bunch of times.
12. While cooking, remove the stems and return the mushrooms to the pot of boiling water.
13. In a soup pot, combine the preserved goji berries and preserved Chinese dates.
14. Over a high flame, bring to the boil.
15. Shave the chicken thighs and set them aside for another pan.
16. Heat a skillet over medium-low heat until it begins to smoke marginally after the soup has boiled for thirty minutes.
17. To coat the skillet, spread the oil all over it.
18. In a soup pot, add the meat. ½ cup water to pan sear the skillet and add it to the casserole dish as well.
19. Season with salt and freshly chopped scallion just before serving.

Chapter 9: Chinese Salad Recipes

MUNG BEAN CLEAR NOODLES CHINESE SALAD

INGREDIENTS

- Coriander, chopped
- Fresh chili, chopped
- 3 tablespoon spicy black bean sauce
- 1 teaspoon black rice vinegar
- 3½ cup water
- ½ cup mung bean starch

COOK TIME: 7 mins
SERVING: 2

INSTRUCTIONS

1. In a mixing bowl, combine ½ cup water and mung bean starch.
2. In a frying pan, heat and cook 3 cups of water until tiny bubbles started to emerge at the bottom.
3. Pour in the flour and water mixture easily with a spoon, stirring continuously.
4. When you see large air bubbles rising to the surface and the liquid appears transparent, remove the pan from the oven.
5. Fill a container halfway with the combination.
6. Allow cooling before refrigerating until it forms a solid paste.
7. Serve with coriander and fresh chili on the side.
8. Black rice is used as a seasoning.

PICKLED CHINESE SALAD

INGREDIENTS

- A small handful of whole cilantro leaves
- 2 teaspoons white sesame seeds
- 2 large garlic cloves
- Red pepper flakes
- 1 teaspoon kosher salt
- 2 teaspoons soy sauce
- 1 tablespoon grapeseed
- 1 ½ tablespoons rice vinegar
- 2 teaspoons sesame oil
- 2 teaspoons granulated sugar

COOK TIME: 40 mins
SERVING: 6

INSTRUCTIONS

1. Cucumbers should be rinsed and dried.
2. Place a cucumber slice cut piece down on a cutting board.
3. Toss the cucumber parts with a large pinch of salt and a large bit of sugar in a colander.
4. Combine the sugar, salt, and rice wine vinegar in a small cup.
5. Stir until the salt and sugar have fully dissolved.
6. Combine the soy sauce and oil in a mixing bowl.
7. When ready to serve, give the cucumbers a good shake to remove any leftover marinade and place them in a serving bowl.
8. Mix thoroughly with cilantro and sesame seeds as a garnish.

GRILLED MUSHROOM AND CHICKEN CHINESE SALAD

INGREDIENTS

- 2 teaspoons sugar
- Salt to taste
- 1 ½ tablespoon lemon juice
- 7-8 black peppercorns
- ½ iceberg lettuce
- Olive oil 1 tablespoon
- 300 grams chicken breast
- 1 medium red capsicum
- 6 black olives stoned and sliced
- 6 large button mushrooms
- Oil 2 tablespoons
- 1 yellow capsicum
- Salt to taste
- ½ teaspoon mustard paste
- ½ teaspoon garlic paste
- ½ teaspoon black pepper powder

COOK TIME: 20 mins
SERVING: 4

INSTRUCTIONS

1. For twenty minutes, caramelize the chicken thighs in salt, spice paste, mustard powder, and fenugreek seeds.
2. To make the dressing, whisk together all of the components.
3. For five to ten minutes on the grill, cook the chicken breasts.
4. Allow cooling before slicing and setting aside.
5. Roast the mushrooms for two minutes after brushing them with oil.
6. Put aside after cutting into pieces.
7. Grill the red and yellow capsicums for ten minutes, rotating once or twice to ensure even cooking.
8. Remove the seeds, cut in the quarter, pick, and set aside.
9. In a big mixing bowl, combine the chicken, onions, bell peppers, olives, and broccoli.
10. Toss the salad in the seasoning to combine it. Serve right away.

CHICKPEA CHINESE SALAD

INGREDIENTS

- 1½ cups small broccoli florets
- ½ cup salted cashews
- 1 cup red bell pepper
- 2 cups red cabbage
- 1 15.5 oz. can chickpeas
- 1 cup shredded carrots
- 1 cup snow peas
- 2 cups cooked quinoa
- **Miso Ginger Dressing**
- 1- 2 teaspoons honey
- ⅛ teaspoon sea salt
- 2 tablespoons gluten-free tamari
- 1 tablespoon rice vinegar
- 1 tablespoon white miso paste
- 1 teaspoon fresh ginger
- 1 tablespoon lemon juice

COOK TIME: 40 mins
SERVING: 4

INSTRUCTIONS

1. Add ½ cup quinoa and ½ cup water in a small saucepan.
2. Get the water to a boil. When boiling, reduce to low heat, cover, and cook for fifteen minutes, or until all of the water has been absorbed.
3. Turn off the heat and allow it to cool for a few minutes after the water has been consumed.
4. In the meantime, prepare the remaining veggies and combine them in a mixing bowl.
5. In a small bowl or fluid quart container, mix all of the ingredients until well mixed.
6. Combine all chopped vegetables, chickpeas, boiled quinoa, and cashew nuts in a big mixing bowl.
7. Toss in the dressing until it is well mixed.

TOFU SHEET AND TOONA SINENSIS SPROUT SALAD

INGREDIENTS

- 1 teaspoon dark soy sauce
- 1 tablespoon cornstarch
- 1 scallion
- 1 tablespoon oyster sauce
- 1 pound firm tofu
- ⅛ teaspoon white pepper
- ¼ teaspoon salt
- 3 oz. ground pork
- 1 teaspoon fresh ginger
- 2 teaspoons Shaoxing wine
- 1 oz. salted fish

COOK TIME: 30 mins
SERVING: 4

INSTRUCTIONS

1. Ground meat and ginger should be minced together.
2. To create room for the pork, scrape out about 1 teaspoon of tofu from each slice.
3. Toss the leftover tofu with the pork in a mixing dish.
4. Toss the meat mixture with the wine, a sprinkle of freshly roasted white pepper, and salt. Mix thoroughly.
5. Toss the meat with the tofu parts and serve.
6. In a skillet or steamer, steam the tofu sheet for about ten minutes.
7. Set aside one tablespoon of cornflour and one tablespoon of water, whereas the tofu is roasting.
8. Remove the plate cautiously when the tofu is finished.
9. Return any remaining water to the skillet and, if necessary, add more water to make around a quarter cup of liquid.
10. Bring the liquid to a low boil, then add the oyster sauce and light sesame oil.
11. Add salt and pepper, then stir in the cornflour liquid.
12. Garnish with spring onions after pouring the sauce over the tofu.

SIRARCHA CHINESE CUCUMBER SALAD

INGREDIENTS

- ¼ to ½ teaspoon granulated sugar
- 1 teaspoon sriracha sauce
- 2 cloves garlic minced
- 1 teaspoon sesame oil
- ½ to 1 teaspoon salt
- 4 Persian cucumbers
- Optional Garnishes
- ¼ teaspoon red pepper flakes
- ½ teaspoon chopped cilantro

COOK TIME: 30 mins
SERVING: 4

INSTRUCTIONS

1. Cucumbers can be cut into parts.
2. Then cut each third laterally in half, and then long ways in half too.
3. Put the cucumbers in a bowl and season with ½ teaspoon salt.
4. Leave them to stay for 30 minutes to allow the salt to pull the water out of the cucumbers.
5. Add in the rest of the ingredients until the cucumbers are completely covered with seasonings.
6. Taste and make any required adjustments.
7. You can eat the cucumbers right away or leave them in the fridge to produce the flavors.

COTTAGE CHEESE CHINESE SALAD

INGREDIENTS

- 2 medium cucumbers
- Salt and pepper to taste
- 4 Roma (plum) tomatoes
- 4 green onions
- 1 container cottage cheese

COOK TIME: 10 mins
SERVING: 4

INSTRUCTIONS

1. Combine the cottage cheese, peppers, fresh basil, and cucumbers in a medium mixing dish.
2. To taste, sprinkle with salt.
3. Chill until ready to serve.

Chapter 10: Most Famous Chinese Dishes

DIM SUMS

INGREDIENTS

- For Chicken and Prawn Dumplings
- Potato starch
- Salt
- 2.5 grams white pepper
- Wonton skin
- 150 grams chicken
- 5 grams sugar
- 5 ml sesame oil
- 150 grams prawn
- For Vegetable Coriander Dumplings
- 5 grams sugar
- 5 grams sesame oil
- 10ml oil
- 10 grams brown garlic
- 10 grams bamboo shoots
- 10 grams garlic
- 10 grams carrots

INSTRUCTIONS

1. Combine sugar, pepper, soy sauce, and cornmeal with minced chicken and prawns.
2. Fill the wonton skin with the combination and steam it.
3. However, for the wanton skin, combine all ingredients.
4. Fill the wonton skin with the mixture and steam it.
5. Combine the potato, 50 gm wheat flour, and a bit of salt in a mixing bowl.
6. Stir in hot water until it the slightly thickened.
7. Add potato starch until it binds.
8. Make a roll and cut it into tiny squares by sprinkling wheat starch on top.
9. Then, using a roller, roll the balls into a flat round or shape before adding fillings.
10. 250g red chilies, soaked for three hours to make a paste out of it.
11. Add chili paste, salt, and sugar once the garlic has turned orange.

- 10 grams water chestnuts
- 10 grams button mushrooms

For Wonton Skin
- 50 grams wheat starch
- Salt
- Potato starch

COOK TIME: 70 mins
SERVING: 4

HOT AND SOUR SOUP

INGREDIENTS

- ½ teaspoon salt
- 2 tablespoon spring onion
- ½ teaspoon pepper powder
- ½ teaspoon sugar
- 2 tablespoon vinegar
- 1 teaspoon chili
- 4 cup water
- 2 tablespoon soy
- 2 tablespoon oil
- ½ capsicum
- 5 beans
- 2 clove garlic
- 1 carrot
- 3 tablespoon cabbage
- 1-inch ginger
- 2 tablespoon spring onion
- 1 chili
- For Corn Flour Slurry
- ¼ cup water
- 2 tablespoon cornflour

COOK TIME: 25 mins
SERVING: 2

INSTRUCTIONS

1. First, heat two tablespoons of oil in a large skillet and stir fry two garlic cloves, 1-inch ginger, and one chili.
2. Mix in 2 tablespoons green onion until it loosens.
3. One carrot, cabbage, ½ capsicum, and five beans are also good additions.
4. Combine the water, sesame oil, vinegar, and chili sauce in a mixing bowl.
5. Add spice powder, salt, and oil as well.
6. Boil for three minutes or until the flavors are well absorbed.
7. To make a cornflour slurry, combine two tablespoons of cornflour with ¼ cup water.
8. Mix the slurry into the broth thoroughly.
9. Boil for another two minutes or until the soup has thickened slightly.
10. Finally, stir in 2 tablespoons green onion and serve the hot and sour broth immediately.

QUICK NOODLES

INGREDIENTS

- 1 medium carrot
- 3 ounces bean sprouts
- 2 garlic cloves
- 2 green onions
- 1 tablespoon soy sauce
- 2 tablespoons vegetable oil
- 3 ounces egg noodles
- 1 tablespoon Shaoxing wine
- 2 teaspoons dark brown sugar
- 1 teaspoon sriracha
- 2 teaspoons sesame oil
- 2 teaspoons dark soy sauce

COOK TIME: 30 mins
SERVING: 2

INSTRUCTIONS

1. Mix sesame oil, dark soy sauce, Shaoxing wine, soy sauce, salt, and sriracha in a small cup. Remove from the heat.
2. A big pot of water should be brought to a boil.
3. Cook the noodles in the broth.
4. Cook for three minutes after adding the noodles.
5. With the remaining one tablespoon oil, bring the skillet to a moderate flame.
6. Sauté the cloves and the white color green parts of the spring onion for about thirty seconds, or until aromatic.
7. Return the noodles, along with the soy sauce mixture, to the pan.
8. Heat for 1 minute more, or until the dark green pieces of the spring onion, carrot ribbons, and black beans are only softened.
9. Switch off the heat and serve.

SZECHUWAN CHILI CHICKEN

INGREDIENTS

- 1 tablespoon black vinegar
- 2 teaspoon chili oil
- 2 teaspoon white pepper
- Oil (for frying)
- 2-3 spring onions
- 10-12 pieces chicken
- to taste salt
- 5-6 dry red chilies
- 3 tablespoon brown peppercorn
- 3 tablespoon green peppercorn
- 2-3 tablespoon ginger

COOK TIME: 45 mins
SERVING: 8

INSTRUCTIONS

1. Cook the chicken in a pan with the ginger until it turns golden.
2. Drain the oil and set it aside for now.
3. Add the onion, fresh basil, green coriander seeds, and dark peppercorns at this stage.
4. Mix in the dry chilies, sesame oil powder, ajino moto, pepper, and chili sauce for five minutes.
5. After another 5-10 minutes of stirring, apply the black vinegar.
6. Stir fry for ten minutes, then serve with green peppercorns as a side dish.
7. Chilli meat Szechwan is ready to eat.

SPRING ROLL

INGREDIENTS

- 3 tablespoons hoisin sauce
- 1 teaspoon peanuts
- 2 ounces rice vermicelli
- 2 tablespoons white sugar
- ½ teaspoon garlic chili sauce
- 8 rice wrappers
- 2 tablespoons fresh lime juice
- 1 clove garlic
- 8 large cooked shrimp
- 4 teaspoons fish sauce
- ¼ cup water
- 1 ⅓ tablespoons Thai basil
- 3 tablespoons cilantro
- 2 leaves lettuce
- 3 tablespoons mint leaves

COOK TIME: 25 mins
SERVING: 6

INSTRUCTIONS

1. A small saucepan of water should be brought to a boil.
2. Three to five minutes, or until al dente, simmer rice vermicelli, and rinse.
3. Fill a large mixing bowl halfway with hot water.
4. To loosen one wrapper, place it in the warm water for 1 second.
5. Add two shrimp halves, a pinch of vermicelli, lettuce, basil, coriander, and cabbage in a row across the middle, keeping about 2 inches exposed on each side.
6. Combine the oyster sauce, water, lemon juice, cloves, sugar, and chili sauce in a small cup.
7. Combine the hoisin paste and peanuts in a separate small dish.
8. Serve the rolled spring rolls with a combination of fish sauce and hoisin sauces.

STIR-FRIED TOFU WITH RICE

INGREDIENTS

- **For the Tofu**
- A handful of coriander leaves
- 1 teaspoon refined oil
- 1-inch red onion, chopped
- 2 teaspoon honey
- 100 grams tofu
- 2 teaspoon soya sauce
- 3 garlic cloves, chopped
- 2 teaspoon chili
- 2 shallots
- 1-inch ginger
- 1 lemongrass stick
- **For the Fried Rice**
- Handful of coriander
- 1 teaspoon olive oil
- 2 teaspoon soya sauce
- ½ lemon (squeezed)
- Carrots, chopped
- 1 fresh red chili, chopped
- 1 ginger
- Salt and pepper
- Spring onions

COOK TIME: 40 mins
SERVING: 4

INSTRUCTIONS

1. In a hot oven pan, rain distilled oil and add minced mariner, stirring well.
2. Then season with salt and pepper and insert the garlic, cloves, and shallots.
3. Combine the red chili paste, sesame oil, and honey in a cup.
4. Put it all together with some coriander.
5. In a hot oven skillet, drizzle vegetable oil and insert carrots, green onions, ginger, salt, and black pepper.
6. Then combine the fresh red chili, lime juice, and soy sauce in a large mixing bowl.
7. Add some cilantro leaves, sliced.
8. Cook for about 5-7 minutes.
9. It is better served on a platter.

SHIITAKE FRIED RICE WITH WATER CHESTNUTS

INGREDIENTS

- Small bunch parsley
- 1 big drop of sesame oil
- A dash of rice wine vinegar
- 1 stalk onions
- 1 cup shitake mushroom
- Pinch white pepper
- 1 big drop of sesame oil
- 1 cup rice (cooked)
- 1 big tablespoon celery
- 1 tablespoon ginger
- 2-3 tablespoon vegetable oil
- ½ medium onion
- 1 big tablespoon of leeks
- Green chilies
- 2-3 water chestnuts
- 4 cloves garlic
- taste

INSTRUCTIONS

1. Cut the water chestnuts, diced peppers, and shitake mushrooms.
2. Vegetable oil is heated in a wok.
3. Combine the onions, kale, and leeks in a large mixing bowl.
4. Grate the ginger, add the mushrooms, and cut the water chestnuts.
5. Combine the rice, green onions, sesame oil, rice vinegar, cloves, and soy sauce in a mixing bowl.
Serve in a bowl after a good stir fry.

COOK TIME: 30 mins
SERVING: 4

CHICKEN WITH CHESTNUTS

INGREDIENTS

- 3 tablespoons hoisin sauce
- 1 teaspoon peanuts
- 2 tablespoons white sugar
- ½ teaspoon garlic chili sauce
- 2 ounces rice vermicelli
- 2 tablespoons fresh lime juice
- 1 clove garlic, minced
- 8 rice wrappers
- 3 tablespoons cilantro
- 2 leaves lettuce
- 4 teaspoons fish sauce
- 1 ⅓ tablespoons Thai basil
- 3 tablespoons mint leaves
- 8 large cooked shrimp
- ¼ cup water

COOK TIME: 50 mins
SERVING: 8

INSTRUCTIONS

1. If needed, cut chicken parts into tiny chunks.
2. Enable chicken to marinate in 2 tablespoons of sesame oil for 10-15 minutes.
3. In a large skillet, heat the oil, add the green onion and ginger, continue cooking until moist.
4. Arrange the chicken parts in a thin layer in the pan.
5. Brown one hand, then flip all of the bits over and brown the other.
6. Add two tablespoons of tomato sauce, sherry, sugar, star anise, soaked in water, shitake mushrooms, and soaking liquid for shitake mushrooms.
7. Combine the sauce and the chicken in a large mixing bowl.
8. Bring to the boil, then decrease to low heat and cook, protected, for 20 minutes.
9. Toss in the chestnuts softly.
10. Cover and continue to cook for an additional 15-20 minutes or until the chicken is soft.

Conclusion

It is no misconception to suggest that "food is a paradise for the citizens" in Chinese. People in China eat tasty food in all sections of life. Cooking has evolved into a complex art form. China is split into 34 provinces, with its rich traditions that reflect its unique landscape, environment, background, and culture. New, local products and seasoning are used to inspire culinary styles. Both of these factors contributed to the creation of the "Eight Delicacies" and "Four Tastes." Crucially, Chinese cuisine is often enjoyed with all of the senses. The presentation and smell of a dish are judged first, followed by the flavor and quality. Moreover, a high-quality dish should have at least one of the following attributes, if not all of them. Chinese Cookbook has a variety of "Chinese Recipes" to choose from. You will have a great chance to experience various local cuisines and improve the taste of your meals at your table.